SEASONS OF THE SOUL

Credit: MJ Magnum

About the Author

Born in Puerto Rico, Sharon M. Koenig is an author, speaker and mother. Her spiritual search began as a way to find answers to overcome a difficult childhood that neither success nor love relationships could ever heal. Before becoming an author, Sharon produced and developed motivational events and personal growth projects for the Latin-American community featuring leaders and bestselling authors from various spiritual backgrounds. She studied about world religions under the direct tutelage of unique spiritual leaders, including a Buddhist lama, a guru from India and a priest. Tolerance and compassion are the guiding lights of her religious language.

Many readers describe Sharon as a writer who can translate profound spiritual lessons into simple and practical terms. She has presented her books, which have an ever-increasing international following, at various bookstores and media venues across the United States, Latin America, and Spain, including CNN Español, Univision, Telemundo and RTVE.es.

She has published three books in Spanish: *Los Ciclos de Alma* (Ediciones Obelisco, Barcelona, 2011), now in its seventh edition; *Las 12 Promesas del Alma* (HarperCollins Español, 2016); and most recently, *Desde Om hasta Amén*, Sharon's memoir about her spiritual journey (HarperCollins Español, 2017).

Sharon volunteers her time and leadership for various wellness and faith community-based projects for mothers and children. She loves gardens, music, traveling, reading, interior decorating, health, lifestyle, philosophy, and nature. She is currently working on various new projects, including children's books. Sharon lives in Miami with her daughter Gabbie and her white Persian cat Michín.

Her goal is to reach and inspire as many people as she can with a vision of a compassionate and inclusive spirituality and to join them in their search for their authentic purpose in life, through a conscious and everlasting connection with God who is unconditionally loving.

www.sharonmkoenig.com
@SharonMKoenigEspanol
@sharonmkoenig
@SharonMKoenig

Praise for *Seasons of the Soul*

'Sharon M. Koenig's book is a great reminder of who we are and why we are here. The reading of her words is already a sweet awakening'

Marianne Williamson, author of *A Return to Love*

'With simple and clear language, Sharon offers us a guide that addresses the complex issue of how to grow our conscience through connection with our spirituality. Her book is truly inspiring in these times of chaos and uncertainty'

Rosa Barocio, author of *Discipline with Love*

'Sharon Koenig has the unique gift of transmitting profound wisdom by engaging in a spontaneous conversation with the reader. Her words find us wherever we are and, at the same time, speak to us from that same place. I adore her honesty, solidarity, and the hope this book contains. I love it. Thanks to her words, I feel closer to God'

Victoria Moran, author of *Living a Charmed Life*

'The Sharon Koenig Connection Process is an invitation to the transformation of our lives. This book is essential for all human beings who want to raise their lives to a spiritual level and learn to operate from that level to allow each master plan to be carried out according to the Divine.

This work is a jewel and a gift of life that ... offers us a practical guide to develop our maximum potential. Sharon Koenig leads us on an inner journey to discover the influence and impact our beliefs and attitudes have on [our] decisions, actions, and results. Her words awaken our conscience, educate and guide us in a simple, easy-to-understand way to imitate and to create a life according to the Divine plan. And [with] the Divine, everything is possible!'

Chris Lee, Transformational Coach and author of *Transform Your Life: 10 Principles of Abundance and Prosperity*

'Thanks to this book full of inspiration, I have learned how to align myself with the forces of the universe to fulfill my true purpose [in] life: to be the voice of those children who cannot speak for themselves'

Jean-Robert Cadet, author of *Restavec*

'This book has everything that is needed to be able to enter the Divine Presence'

Muñeca Geigel, author of *The Art of Being Happy*

'Sharon has the gift of leading people to connect with their Divinity'

Judy Brooks, producer of the PBS TV show *Healing Quest*

SEASONS OF THE SOUL

7 Steps to Connect with Your Life's Highest Purpose

SHARON M. KOENIG

PAN

This edition first published 2021 by Pan
an imprint of Pan Macmillan Publishing India Private Limited
707 Kailash Building
26 K. G. Marg, New Delhi 110001
www.panmacmillan.co.in

Pan Macmillan, 6 Briset St, Farringdon, London EC1M 5NR
Associated companies throughout the world
www.panmacmillan.com

ISBN 978-81-949707-3-6

English language edition for the Indian Subcontinent only arranged through Montse Cortazar Literary Agency (www.montsecortazar.com).

Originally published in Spanish as *Los Ciclos del Alma: El Proceso de Conexión, Un Camino para Tu Verdadero Propósito* by Ediciones Obelisco, Barcelona, in 2011

1 3 5 7 9 8 6 4 2

Although the messages in the book can relieve the soul, its contents cannot diagnose or replace any medical or professional treatment or advice. Before starting a new routine of spiritual or physical exercises, always consult your doctor or therapist. Never interrupt medications or treatments without proper medical supervision. Please, in the case of depression, either yours or that of someone close to you, and especially when you notice that there are suicidal thoughts or inability to manage emotions, go immediately to a family member and seek professional help. These behaviors reflect an emergency, and you should resort to immediate assistance.

Typeset in Sabon LT Std by R. Ajith Kumar, New Delhi
Printed and bound in India by Replika Press Pvt. Ltd.

For my God, who inspires me, and my daughter Gabrielle, who blesses me with her presence every day

For my grandmother Amparo, who planted the seeds of spirituality in my heart, and for Dada, a holy man from India who showed me the face of God

CONTENTS

PROLOGUE

AS I FINISH TRANSLATING THESE WORDS, A NEW PANDEMIC is threatening our world. It has been just over 100 years since the Spanish Flu pandemic brought extreme chaos to our world in 1918. When our outside world seems to be on the brink of collapse, we have no other alternative but to reach inside ourselves for answers. This book is a reminder that life travels in cycles, sometimes the cycles are so far apart that we can no longer remember when the last one paid us a visit. Fortunately, as the seasons of life continue their journey, the past teaches that the good times are only a stone's throw away from returning. After the darkness of the night, there's always a morning and a sunrise which overcome it and cast out the darkness.

Reflecting on the times, I told my daughter not worry, these are the stories we hear from those who were fortunate enough to live to tell the tale. The gift of living a long life comes with everything that makes our experiences meaningful. Listen to the centenarians, and they will tell you about wars, losses, and financial depressions, but they will also tell you about love, laughter, and the immense joy of living. As Martin Luther King Jr. once said, 'Only when it's dark enough can you see the stars.'[1]

As I write the introduction to this English edition of my book, I can't help but be overwhelmed with gratitude. The original Spanish version of *Seasons of the Soul* was first published in Barcelona in 2011 as *Los Ciclos del Alma* and quickly became a bestseller. Since the original publication, several editions have been printed and distributed in various countries. You never know where a book will take you, and *Seasons of the Soul* has certainly surprised me with an unexpected journey.

The most significant gift as an author is the positive feedback we receive from our readers. I am so very pleased to hear that after nine years the book continues to be at their bedside, a place more sacred than the shelves of the best bookstore.

As I translate the words to English I am amazed to find that *Seasons of the Soul* is especially relevant to our times and has proven to be somewhat prophetic. The world is experiencing growing pains, and considering the current political and social situation, we need an invitation to tolerance, consolation, and hope.

I never intended to be a spiritual writer, far from it. I began my journey in the fast-paced world of the fashion business, where I tried to heal unresolved childhood trauma by self-medicating with personal attachments and accomplishments. However, it was not long before I realized that people and material success were not

---

[1] From 'I've Been to the Mountaintop' (1968), Dr. King's final speech before his assassination.

permanent means to find healing. Through the process of discovery, I accidentally became what sages from the East call a 'seeker', devoting more than thirty years to learning the secrets of spirituality. People from a wide variety of places and beliefs all became my teachers; be they alchemists, lamas, metaphysicians, magicians, monks, best-selling authors, shamans, philosophers, pastors, priests, business acquaintances, and indigenous people from a wide variety of places and beliefs. These teachings came to me from faraway places such as India, Tibet, England, North America, and South America, and as near to my soul as the mountains of my own Puerto Rico, the land of my birth. Everyone I met and interacted with had a different language to connect with God. In the end, we all describe the Divine according to our own experiences and upbringing.

I also learned valuable lessons from unlikely people I encountered along my journey – some who appeared to be quite simple yet harbored great wisdom within. I have gained valuable insights from every person I have loved, as well as from a few I have wanted to forget.

Not unfrequently, the spiritual disciplines I have learned seemed too difficult to practice. Some demanded costly courses of meditations and altered levels of consciousness. Countless lessons became complicated lectures, filled with confusing theology. I yearned for a simpler way to connect spiritually. I soon realized that although some positive thinking techniques were effective, the results were not always reliable – our heart's desire does not always correlate with our highest good or that of the people around us. Despite the attainment of our desires through positive thinking, I saw that the emptiness remained. Even when we received what we wanted, the happiness still depended on an outside source resulting in attachment, better known as 'the fear of losing the newfound way to fill the void'. This newfound external source of love, approval, or security was too unpredictable and forever changing – leading to temporary joy, followed by repeated relapses into the same original void and negative behavioral pattern of attachment, anxiety, fear, and loss. This cycle of getting up, attaining, and falling again was my experience year after year. Even with the awareness that the only way to find true harmony was by allowing God's love to manifest in my life, in real-life practice, I did not know how to keep the connection for too long, experiencing what I called a 'fall'. One day, as I was experiencing one of those 'falls', I remembered a simple lesson from Dada[2], a teacher and guru from India whom I had met through a mutual business friend. I wanted to know what the secret was. Specifically, I wanted to understand what went wrong with my experiment with the secret laws of the universe. To these questions, he would always respond, with a humble smile and pointing his index finger to the sky: 'God is the secret.' Dada was the teacher who curiously inspired me to return to my original tradition by introducing me to a personal and loving God. I finally integrated his message, adding God back into the equation of my dreams.

The answers to your riddles lie within you. No one can really 'educate' you. The word 'educate' comes from the Greek word *educere*, which means 'to bring forth what you

---

[2] Dada J.P. Vaswani, a noted spiritual leader from India, was the head of the Sadhu Vaswani Mission.

already have within'; thus, no teacher is indispensable. I don't trust the modality of motivation, adrenaline is not a permanent solution. Adrenaline can help if you need to run for your life, but it is not a reliable source of fuel for the long run. Life was not meant to be a nonstop marathon, especially if we are running from ourselves. I've learned that no one can motivate someone to do something he or she is not destined to do in their lives, at least not for long. Does the flower need a reason to bloom? Does the rain need a reason to fall on parched ground? If we need constant motivation to continue on a path, we may need to ask ourselves if this is the right direction. I prefer to use the word 'inspire', which comes from *spirare*, meaning 'to breathe'. We can always invite God to reveal our purpose.

The big question is: How do I get to that point? In other words: How can I discover the obstacles that keep me from experiencing fully who I already am?

The path towards peace is one of inner reflection and observation that is born out of a conscious and voluntary connection with your true inner Self and God. When I say 'God', I do it for lack of a better word that can be understood by all.

The name of God can be confusing since it is commonly associated with fear, judgment, guilt, punishment, and even war, the reason so many have turned away from His guidance. God is the intelligence beyond comprehension that brings order to a seemingly chaotic world. He unifies everything in one giant breath of love. God is omnipresent and omniscient. He is ever-loving, forgiving, just, and universal. I have found that these seemingly abstract qualities by no means deter us from experiencing Him in a personal way. We all dwell in Him, the same way He dwells in us, or as Paul noted in the book of Acts: 'In God we live, move, and have our being ... We are His offspring.'

I am not one to judge individual religions or beliefs. God is one, and each religion has its own particular language. I believe God has a plan for the healing of all humanity and has revealed Himself uniquely throughout every culture across time. We cannot say that all religions are the same; there are special symbols and unique ways of communicating with divinity. I believe these codes were given to humans as a reference and not as a weapon to hurt one another or to divide us over the truth of one belief over the other. Let us all remember that His power is already embracing you, and no matter what you call Him or Her, God is only a call away from manifesting in your life. God is One, regardless of your religion, color, or location. He is all you need to live in the light. When we connect to His Will and His eternal, compassionate, omnipresent, and intelligent strength, we no longer need to chase after mistaken dreams or manifest desires through techniques, decrees, or laws. The rightful dreams will simply come to you in unimaginable ways. When you live in this constant connection, you will realize that your highest expression and true purpose in life will spontaneously and inevitably reveal itself at the right moment. Remember, you are resting within the same wisdom that orchestrates all the galaxies of the universe. This alignment with goodness is our natural state of being, but it has become oxidized by our fears, doubts, resentments, and the false illusion that separates us from His true wisdom. We are disconnected from His source by our wrong beliefs and unwillingness to yield to His order. In other words, we turn away from his love every time we forget who we truly are.

How to use this book

This book is an instruction manual to awaken the soul. I have written it as a conversation, much like the ones I had with the many teachers who taught me, as well as other seekers. My intention is to share the universal teachings that still stand the test of time when it comes to practicality. Instead of rules to follow, orthodoxy and theology, I will share life-changing lessons of spirituality, together with universal values and real-life practices. In truth, you do not need to do anything special except read the book with your full attention.

Seasons of the Soul is about the essence of the lessons I learned. Speaking to thousands of spiritual seekers over the years, I realized that we all need something practical. And I made it a point to simplify the complicated lessons. Sometimes, a spiritual conversation is all it takes to help someone shift from despair to hope. It wasn't long before I discovered that if I consistently followed certain steps, miracles would spontaneously happen in the lives of the people I was trying to help, as well as my own. Seeing all the weight lifted from their shoulders after our conversations, I would sit and review all the steps we had followed before the transformation took place. And when I say transformation or miracle, I am referring to a change of perception, the process of overcoming negative experiences of the past or experiencing a drastic, spontaneous realization harmoniously and without extensive suffering. There are no magic potions for spiritual healing, and indeed it is not a substitution for professional therapy, which I also receive and recommend in moments of need. Yet, there are steps that we can take to live a joyful life. Peace is not so much the result of resolving an issue, but the acceptance and willingness to let go of a hurtful interpretation. The solution for most of our dilemmas will reveal itself in as much as we are willing to allow Divine intervention.

The steps I practice follow a particular order, which begins with a moment of voluntary self-observation, acceptance, and gratitude, before experiencing a 'shift'. This spontaneous change is the result of a voluntary connection to the Divine, that automatically induces healing through forgiveness. Some may call it a spiritual awakening or metanoia, the Greek word for a change of mind. I noticed that in this state dreams became a reality for many. The goals ranged from a job offer to an award and a reconciliation; from obtaining citizenship to a love relationship or even receiving spontaneous healing. More significant, was seeing that inner peace and harmony remained regardless of external conditions, and the dramas of life began to subside. At times, the solution to a problem can be right in front of us, but our resistance, lack of forgiveness, and distraction with things from the past can blind us. As the well-known gospel song 'Amazing Grace' says, 'I was blind, but now I see.' What a great description of a moment of awakening. I could no longer deny the obvious connections; there was something special to this sequence. After practicing the same steps again and again with the same results, I wanted to share the process with everyone, and for a decade, it has helped many, myself included.

Within these pages, you will find what I call the Connection Process, a sequence of seven lessons that I've found to be the most helpful in clearing the path towards peace. I would suggest you read them in order without skipping chapters since each lesson prepares the way towards the final insight. As you read through these pages, I pray you spontaneously experience a new awareness, allowing yourself to reach a healthier perception of the different areas of your life. Sometimes the best solution to a problem is learning to see with 'new eyes'. If we ask God to be able to see afresh, He will answer with a new and corrected vision of an old dilemma. The lessons are simple but they are filled with insights. If you have walked in the spiritual path long enough, many teachings will be familiar to you. This process is not about finding a temporary solution; it is about providing ourselves with tools for a new way of life. There will be lots of reflection and some writing exercises; may I suggest a journal or any kind of notebook you can divide into sections. I look forward to spending the next few weeks with you as we journey together.

INTRODUCTION

THE BEGINNING OF OUR COMMUNION WITH GOD IS TO 'know thyself', as the Greek aphorism reminds us. One of the best ways I've found to help us learn about ourselves is by observing how nature behaves. Nature moves in cycles. In the context of this book, a season is a spiritual metaphor for the observation of the qualities displayed in different moments of our lives. A cycle is a periodic manifestation through which everything evolves in the universe, while the seasons are the outward display. As the seasons return every year, we can see a pattern, and to some extent, we can even predict them. A cycle moves in rhythms that suggest a grand spiral as opposed to a closed circle since there is always an opening to start fresh again. In the great journey of life, nothing returns to its place of origin without experiencing transformation.

Hurricanes, galaxies, and atoms each have their orbits. Their unique cycles lasting either one microsecond or an apparent eternity, depending on our point of reference. The instant sequence of an atom could be compared to a hundred journey years of a galaxy moving in what appears to be a spiral. There are macrocycles, such as the planets' journeys through the heavens, and microcycles, like the orbit of the moon, which affects the sea and even feminine cycles. Everything in the universe is evolving in this manner. We are all part of this circadian timer, connected in a compulsory pattern that echoes itself throughout the universe. Each cycle is part of a unity, a mutual harmony.

I am not pretending to give a science dissertation; a simple act of observing nature can teach us a lot about who we are. We can only describe what we see with our physical eyes, and in our daily lives, we are only conscious of some of the cycles, but there's so much more. The search for God began with the observation of the stars and their cycles. Different cultures calculate eras in thousands and even millions of years.

Every religion has its own creation story, an attempt to explain with a metaphor what cannot be solved by reason. As a scientific interpretation of the Catholic tradition's creation story of 'In the beginning, there was the light', we have the Big Bang Theory – initially proposed by Georges Lemaitre, a Jesuit Catholic priest. In Hindu philosophy, the universe is a manifestation of Brahma, the 'All' who performs an eternal grand dance of creation and destruction by the god Shiva, only to begin anew. In this cosmology, the universe expands and contracts, which explains the universe's capacity to create and destroy itself. Hindu cosmologists and the Bhagavad Gita divide these inhalations and exhalations of the universe into eras or predictable cycles called *yugas*. They replay themselves over millions of years, according to their teachings.

Many cultures and religions agree that there was a separation, and that we are in the midst of a return.

Spirituality is thus better defined as *the way back home* – it is not surprising that most spiritual practices are defined as a path. First Christians were known as people who 'belonged to the Way',[3] the Tao means path, way or road. In Hinduism, there is the concept of the Eternal Way, in Buddhism, we find the Middle Way. Some also mention guidance within the path, words like Dharma, the Law, the way of salvation. They all look forward to a final destination or a spiritual state, known by some as heaven, moksha or nirvana.

Some traditions also prophesy a cataclysmic or fateful end to the world as we know it. I, for that matter, do not encourage pessimistic beliefs about apocalyptic endings. Conversely, if we remember that the word 'apocalypse' means revelation, seeing everything with new eyes will be a better outcome. According to Buddhism, we live in a world of maya, or the illusion that causes suffering, suggesting that the lifting of this veil will free us. Some indigenous traditions call this illusion 'The Dream'. In Christianity, we have the words of John: 'And ye shall know the truth, and the truth shall make you free.'[4]

We don't need to wait until the end of time to start this process. With each answer, a new question will be born, but one fact is clear: We are questioning our assumptions about everything we considered to be the norm, with a voice that grows louder by the day. We are wondering who we are and challenging the status quo from finances to human rights, from medicine and spirituality to education

---

[3] Acts 9:2

[4] John 8:32

and government. The instant availability of information throughout the internet has made the process of finding answers more democratic, and at the same time, more confusing. In this new cycle, we won't be able to overlook social injustices any longer. The last decade was about becoming aware of the contradictions in our society; I predict the next ones will be about action and change.

Even when many are lost in the world, dazzled by the great circus of distractions, we can't deny injustice any longer. Especially when what is truly important for all is compromised for the benefit of a few. Instead, we need to make an effort to seek balance and wellness for all. If we do not, the universe will do it for us. We will not be able to ignore the imbalance we've created in the environment. We have awoken to the fact that changes in nature for the worse are not a myth but the consequence of living off-balance. To remain indifferent, choosing to believe that life as we know it will stay the same without us having to change our ways, will only cause more harm. A cell in the human body cannot have a plan of its own – it must follow a universal design. In the same manner, you cannot have a plan of your own without including 'The All'. There's a perfect order, one that we disrupt as we hold on to unconscious desires that do not consider a harmonious design.

It is illogical to pretend to coordinate all the details of the universe. We'll only end up exhausted as we struggle to control our lives and the lives of others, micromanaging the universe without Divine assistance. Our job is not to manage the universe but to allow God to express his love to the world through each one of us. The consequence of not finding our purpose is confusion, dissatisfaction, depression, financial problems, and illnesses. We need to continue to ask essential questions about who we are, where we come from, and why we are here. True, we might not always find answers, yet the questions will be enough to propel us to search for a life of meaning.

Studies of happiness and longevity around the world have found that the most important variable regarding a positive outcome of their health, is whether people have found their purpose. Those who have found their 'reason to get up in the morning', or *ikigai* as it's called in Japan, are joyful doing what they love while offering their talents to the community and the world. Every culture has a version of a balanced and meaningful way of life; in Japan, this is called ikigai, in the Danish tradition, *hygge* means a feeling of contentment or well-being, while the Swedish have *lagom*, meaning 'just the right amount'.

We may forget our purpose at times, but our soul doesn't forget; it always reminds us through a 'certain emptiness' we cannot fill no matter what we acquire or achieve.

This book is a calling, a reminder, and an invitation to enlist yourself in the plan that God has designed specifically for you. No one can occupy your position; you are indispensable in God's plan. To learn our mission, we need to connect directly with Him. The connection to the higher wisdom of God requires a conscious and voluntary effort.

Your true purpose is recognized only by the fulfilling happiness you feel at those fleeting moments when you are connected and engaged in your right work. The authentic purpose gives you and those around you the gift of a higher good for all.

We cannot change the oscillations of cycles; we cannot control the seasons. However, we can learn to identify the storms and navigate through turbulent waters. We cannot avoid winter, but we can prepare for its arrival, supplying ourselves with food, warm clothes, and shelter. We cannot control the highs and lows of the tides, but we can learn the coordinates and keep our course without losing sight of our true north.

PART I

THE ESSENCE OF MAN

1

WHO ARE YOU?

IN A FAST-PACED WORLD, WE DEMAND EXCELLENCE, efficiency, and productivity. We are eager to reach our goals quickly, yet how many of us take the time to ask ourselves: Where am I going and why? These are timely questions that will eventually guide us to deeper ones, such as: What is the meaning of everything? What are the rules of the game in life? Am I truly happy? How do I measure happiness? On the other hand, a wrong answer will lead us to a never-ending road of disappointment.

We are stardust

Once during a visit to the New York City Museum of Natural History with my daughter, I marveled at the astonishing display of galaxies and wondered about my purpose in this infinite universe. I questioned my significance as just a tiny dust particle in the middle of a never-ending universe. Then I remembered that the smallest of living organisms, like cells, bacteria, and even parasites, has its grand purpose. Each one is indispensable to the evolution of life on our planet, where they all follow a previously designed plan.

One universal principle states, 'As above, so below', meaning the design of the universe repeats itself at different degrees and levels of existence. Imagine for a moment that we can look at the things around us from the perspective of a subatomic particle. We would probably see everything – tables, people, water – not as physical objects, but precisely as I saw the galaxies at the planetarium, as an immense space, a great void with tiny particles, as planets and stars. In physics, the only difference between a rock and a leaf is their atomic configuration and vibration. The faster the vibration, the less visible the object; the slower the vibration, the denser it looks. Gases vibrate faster than solids. We are made of the same stuff. We are all one: only one body of matter and only one spirit that animates everything.

> *Everything we call real is made of things that cannot be regarded as real.*
>
> — Niels Bohr

In moments of reflection I wonder what the universe would look like if I could see it from the perspective of a cell looking at a human body. What kind of shape would it look like to me? Would the universe look like a gigantic human being? Like God's actual image? Or would it look just like me, only in His image and likeness?

We are much like the stars in the heavens, unaware of being part of a majestic solar system. Just like us, each star is part of The All. We cannot delete a star from the sky – it cannot be surgically removed or destroyed. A star can only be transformed by becoming part of another at the end of its cycle, and stars can also become part of us.

God loves things by becoming them.

— Richard Rohr

As Pierre Teilhard de Chardin reminded us, 'We are not human beings having a spiritual experience; we are spiritual beings having a human experience.' When I speak of the soul, I am referring to the true Self, that part of us that touches the Divine, that lives beyond the body. We all are souls (simultaneously) living a physical experience. Earth is our school, but not our permanent home. To travel here, to this alien habitat, we had to obtain a garment, a temporary suit made of the earth substance with all the features necessary to survive in this foreign and harsh environment. Notice that 'Adam' means 'made from the earth'. We needed a physical body for movement, a mind to create and discern, emotions to feel and protect us, and an ego to create an individual identity. We are a physical version of the soul, adapted to this Earth, perfectly prepared to face the world we were born into, to live, grow, love, and learn.

In the same way, if we wanted to dive to the bottom of the sea, we would need special diving gear to survive in this new environment. Once back above the water, we would not need the diving gear any longer and would simply discard it. We may apply the same idea to the body, our 'diving gear' during this existence on Earth.

The problem arises when we forget who we are, identifying ourselves with the temporary and confusing the gear with our true eternal inner Self.

The illusion among us

Fear is the opposite of love, and the worst enemy of love is the illusion of divisiveness – believing that we are separate beings is the big lie. The ego deceives us with the fear of losing our source of love, but we cannot lose the essence of what we already are. We have forgotten that we are all part of one body. It's not possible to cause pain to another without hurting ourselves. Unsurprisingly, the meaning of the Greek word *diabolos* is division. Love and fear cannot coexist.

> *There is no fear in love. But perfect love drives out fear because fear has to do with punishment. The one who fears is not made perfect in love.*
>
> — 1 John 4:18

A Course in Miracles summarized the meaning of the above passage in the now immortalized phrase: 'Love is letting go of fear.' In other words, nothing can touch that which is made perfect in love. Shadows are not real. God is light, and darkness is only a perception. Conversely, *awareness* is our ability to see things uncorrupted. The recognition of unity will conquer all divisiveness. The real meaning of the word *enlightenment* is to be able to see the world as it is.

Interconnection: Nature's way

Nature is the best teacher of unity. It shows us how to work together and in harmony. One day while I was visiting a forest in Puerto Rico, a friend brought to my attention the strength of the tabonuco tree. These trees are strong and tall like the highest cathedrals, yet they can withstand winds from the most destructive hurricanes. What is their secret? On the surface, the trees appear to be isolated and separate from one another. Yet, we have discovered they are all holding one another by their big roots – like the long arms of a giant octopus. They embrace each other forever connected in a chain of love. These trees are interdependent, sharing the nutrients of the Earth through loving arms that interconnect, giving them the strength that makes them practically invincible. I even noticed a fallen tree nearby that was still healthy and green, because it was connected to the others.

The grand theater of life

When we receive our 'diving gear' to come to Earth, we also accept the character we will play in the theater of life. We learn life lessons through this fiction since the play is the great school that teaches us through these illusory dramas, recreated and performed as if they were real. The problem arises when we confuse this imaginary world with what is true – when we mistake the character for the actor and the drama for reality.

Maya, a Sanskrit word that means illusion, teaches about the confusion we experience when we believe the theater play to be the reality and our temporary character to be our identity. It is only upon returning to our authentic home, without costumes or masks, that we finally become aware of our true nature. We cannot become attached or identify ourselves with things, beliefs, or situations in this world since they are only part of this transitory stage.

> *The world and its desires pass away, but whoever does the will of God lives forever.*
>
> — 1 John 2:17

The people we love – our fathers, our mothers, our children, and even those we believe to be our enemies – are all made of spirit. Beyond their temporary theater character, they will be with us forever because they are also part of God.

Things are not always as they seem

One essential practice I have learned is to look at life events from the unattached perspective of 'the great observer' or our true Self. This demands we look at the situation from a neutral point of view with the awareness that things are not always as we believe them to be. Instead of reacting, it will be beneficial to watch the events from a neutral perspective – without euphoria (extreme happiness) and without despair (unleashed sadness) – remaining centered, without judgment or expectations, and in total acceptance of the present. It is to understand that the same higher intelligence that orchestrates all events in this universe is always working with you as well. When we live in constant connection to God's Will, we have no choice but to trust that God is working towards our highest good. It is futile to try to draw our own conclusions about what we see in moments of confusion. Our senses and first impressions can deceive our perception and judgments. It is better to take a pause and allow the natural development of the events to show us the truth.

GOOD OR BAD? ONLY GOD KNOWS

There is a well-known Taoist story about a wise farmer who lived with his only son in a small town. One of their few possessions was an old horse that they used to bring their harvest to the market. One night, a massive storm struck the village. The next day, the farmer woke to find his horse had escaped. A curious neighbor approached him and said sadly: 'It is terrible that you have lost your horse!'

To this statement, the wise man responded, 'Good or bad, only God knows.' The neighbor looked at him in confusion and went on his way, scratching his head.

The following day, the wise farmer noticed that his horse had returned and, to his surprise, had also brought along several wild horses. The curious neighbor approached him again and commented with much joy, 'How lucky for you, my friend! You will now turn rich by selling all those horses!' To the neighbor's surprise, the wise man replied one more time, 'Good or bad, only God knows.'

The next day, the farmer's son began to train the wild horses. Unfortunately, he was thrown from one of the wild horses and broke his leg in the fall. Again, came the curious neighbor and told the farmer with much concern: 'How upsetting, my friend, that this should happen to your son since he is your only help. Now you will lose everything because the wild horses won't benefit you. They'll only eat all the food without giving you anything in return.'

The stoic and wise man answered, 'Good or bad? Only God knows.' The neighbor looked at him in disbelief again and, feeling insulted, left muttering about the farmer's absurd reply.

The following day, news arrived that a dangerous war had erupted, and the king's delegates were searching door-to-door for the youngest villagers to send to the war front. They recruited all the young ones in the village, but when they came to the farmer's house, they left his son behind since, given his accident, he was of no use in the war.

Everyone at the village was astounded, including the questioning neighbor, yet the wise farmer simply repeated what he had said from the beginning, 'Good or bad? Only God knows.'

This story perfectly shows how everything is relative; what seems to be a disgrace may turn out to be a blessing in disguise and vice versa. When something or someone comes to you with a message, be neutral because it may be true or not. It may be positive or temporarily negative. Only time will tell.

~

Our true Self is polluted by all the identities, habits, and beliefs acquired throughout the years. Instead of learning something new, we should do consider the exact opposite: unlearn most of the information we have received; in other words, *deprogram ourselves of what we are not*.

You are not your body

Our body is only a 'diving gear'. Still, without it your soul would not be able to walk on this Earth. Therefore, it is our responsibility to care for our bodies by providing a proper diet, adequate exercise, rest, oxygen, and energy. However, our bodies may also demand other things it may not need in excess, for example, caffeine, alcohol, unhealthy sex, etc. It is important to remember that you control your body and not the other way around. The same is true for your thoughts and emotions, which are part of the 'diving gear' as well and should not be allowed to control your real Self.

Many people mistakenly identify with their bodies. They succumb to obsessions and harmful extremes, striving to reach a perceived perfection that is nothing more than an image they believe others will find acceptable. They fail to realize that what they perceive to be beautiful is most likely defined by the culture, fashion, or the fad of the moment. To have the body of a model out of a Rubens painting or that of a Degas ballet dancer is not important. What matters is that both are beautiful art; nevertheless, real and lasting beauty only emanates from within.

You are not your beliefs

Have you ever asked yourself how you came to think the way you do or why you dress the way you dress? How did you come to agree with a specific political party or not?

Where did your lifestyle preferences originate? Why are you attracted to a specific group of people and yet, repelled by others? From a very young age we hear and adopt as our own, the dominant thoughts according to our society. We learn how to think from the people who represent authority in our lives – family members, teachers, and peers at school become our examples of how to react and how to judge. Their views might not be the correct way to see reality since there is not a single way, but rather thousands of ways to see the world. An idea that we have heard enough can become a belief. Most of us do not live authentic lives since subconsciously we choose things, situations, and beliefs that will guarantee those around us will accept us.

You are not what you do

We live our lives in seasons. In some chapters of our story we are the children, and in others, we are the parents. In many instances, we tend to confuse our true Self with the role we have in that particular season. When we adopt these identities, being the father, the businessman, or the caretaker, we believe we are those identities. We continually confuse what we do with who we are. We are much more than those temporary roles; we are the 'great immutable observers' – looking at the film of our lives through a series of seasons and chapters.

You are neither what you do, nor what you have, nor what you think. You are a soul that is loved by God beyond accomplishments and duties.

Case closed

Perhaps the greatest lesson I have received about the end of our days comes from nursing homes. My mother suffers from Alzheimer's. Given her lack of memory, each moment is entirely new for her. As a consequence, when I am with her, the moment becomes new for me as well, since no matter how special the previous occasion, she forgets them all – a lesson on being present. The positive side is that she can't remember the sad parts of her life either. Those who left and those who harmed her in her past – are all gone from her memory. Most of our suffering is a result of unresolved memories of our personal history. What impresses me most during my visits to nursing homes is seeing how even in their old age; some people still show their attachments to their past roles. The thought that we repeated long enough can become crystallized in an automatic pattern and can end up in a case of mania. While I was trying to find a safe nursing home for my mother, I had the opportunity to observe many examples where this was the case. For instance, a lady who happened to be a judge before retiring got my attention. She identified with her power and role so seriously that even after many years in retirement, she still played the part of the fearsome judge in the nursing home. As a result, she always sat alone, never losing her stern look. Her ways reflected her life and how she chose to live it – alone and feared. Case closed.

Stories like this make me realize that none of the recognitions, the properties, or the honors we get are of any value at that point. What matters at the end of life is not what we kept, but what we gave. In contrast to this story, I've met another elder who was very humble and loving; you just wanted to hug her. She had early dementia, but I noticed a photo in her dining room and realized she was one of the founding members of a prominent community organization.

The main questions at the end of our life will be: Did we leave a legacy behind? Did we leave the world a better place for future generations? Did we love? Did we serve others? At the end of our days, what truly counts is the small or big acts of love we did for others – the true meaning of transcendence.

You are not an island

Most of our prejudices arise from the invisible lines that divide our planet into different geographical areas, segregating the organic diversity of dialects, cultures, races, beliefs, and colors. These imaginary divisions lead us to the mistaken belief that our birthplace dictates what is right concerning the rest of the planet.

Do you ever stop to think that there are thousands of cultures in the world? Countless ways of thinking, of dressing, of living. We forget that there is a variety of people on the other side of the world: Buddhists, Hindus, Christians, Muslims, all beings of different skin colors, features, languages, dialects, and customs.

One useful exercise is to imagine yourself at airports in different countries, watching travelers as they come and go. Picture thousands of people walking towards their respective destinies, dressed in different attire and with very different features. Heathrow Airport in London, England, comes to mind. It is a carousel of different native dresses in colors and races of every part of the world. I wonder if Heaven will be any different.

Have you observed your thoughts when you see someone different from you? Say you are white; what do you think about an indigenous or black person? If you are an American, what do you think about Europeans? What do you think of an Asian or Arabic person? Say you are financially disadvantaged; what do you think of a rich man? And if you are rich, what do you think of a poor man?

Keep in mind that whatever you think of people different from you, whether good or bad, is still a judgment.

Are you indeed 'cultured'?

During a dinner conversation, I overheard an upper-class person refer to 'cultured' people as superior and civilized, meaning educated in prestigious universities and with financial means. At that moment, an image came to mind: An educated person might laugh at someone who lives in a remote place, away from the advances of civilization, for not being able to turn on an electric stove. In contrast, the native person might laugh at the 'civilized' one for not being able to light a fire. The native would probably call this 'civilized' person 'uncultured'. Undoubtedly, a genuinely cultured person is the one with an open mind, capable of learning with authentic curiosity and interest both from royalty and humble beginnings. Both worlds have a specific culture unique to their lifestyle and region.

There cannot exist a culture that tries to be exclusive.
— Mahatma Gandhi

New York City is a melting pot of people from all over the world. Living there taught me a lot about tolerance. Reaching out to others takes effort. When taking taxis in New York City, I discreetly look at the driver's last name on his displayed license. If it ends in Singh, I have learned that the driver is probably a Sikh, and one of their masters is Guru Nanak, a saint from India. Other times if I encounter a Muslim driver, I ask about their prayers. When you show any interest in another, their faces light up. You would feel the same way if you were a minority, and someone treated you in this manner.

Whether he is the Pakistani owner of the store in your neighborhood or the Chinese waiter at your favorite restaurant; the next time someone who is different from you crosses your path, share something with him. They are human beings just like you, and if you give them a chance, you will be surprised to find out how similar you are to each other. We all have the same fears, the same problems with our children, the same concerns, and insecurities. That is the real essence of the universal lesson: we are one.

PRACTICE: YOU ARE NOT ALONE, RECOGNIZING GOD IN EVERY PERSON

You can practice being present during your day-to-day life. For example, look at the waiter serving you in a restaurant, don't look at him just as your server; look at him from the perspective of oneness. When you speak to another person, look him in the eyes; the windows of the soul can show a lot about a person. Notice that just like you, this being is on a similar journey and might have the same problems. He may have children, surely a mother and a father. Look at him with empathy and think: 'I am a part of God; God is within me and also within you. We are equal.' It is easy to love someone familiar to you, not as comfortable with someone who looks different. It doesn't help that we have been trained to be afraid of strangers yet becoming aware of the divinity of another is the most powerful practice you can learn. In India, the greeting *namaste* means 'I bow to the Divine in you.'

Tolerance does not necessarily mean that we need to agree or share beliefs with another, as long as we don't cross each other's boundaries. We need to come to terms that everyone has a right to their views, and they may very well be different from yours. We show respect for others when we are willing to listen without judgment. We open our arms to peace whenever we take a genuine interest in learning from another culture and their customs. War, conflict, abuse, and competition arise from not understanding that if the other person or side doesn't get ahead, neither will you.

You are not what you know

Some will argue that there is only one truth, their truth. However, there are many levels of understanding of any truth; our comprehension changes according to context, ability, consciousness, and even the instruments that are available in a particular culture or time. You might look at your hands and see them as empty, whereas a microscope would reveal bacteria and the like. And as a result of greater awareness, today, everyone is washing their hands.

When searching for the truth, openness is more important than accuracy. Some groups believe they have the absolute truth, while others accept any truth without question. However, a truth is not a truth if it cannot be challenged. Most of us have been 'self-domesticated'. To survive, we have adapted our beliefs and behavior to a particular group or environment. Ever since childhood and school, we have learned to accept adults' authority and concepts without challenging them. Even when we don't agree, we keep silent to avoid confrontation or, worse, the risk of losing the approval of peers.

We need to dare to go beyond the story we've been told since others might have a perspective of life we have not yet seen.

My dear friend and once mentor Puerto Rican author Muñeca Geigel, now in Heaven, once told me this valuable story about the power of questioning the truth:

HOW MUCH CAN YOUR MIND HOLD?

Once there was a family that had passed its baked tenderloin recipe from generation to generation. The recipe specified that two inches needed to be cut from the end of the tenderloin before seasoning. For generations, the family dutifully followed these instructions, since the recipe demanded that no steps be changed to guarantee the flavor. Then one day, a young family member, curious enough to question the recipe, asked why they needed to cut two inches from the tenderloin. She didn't understand how that could affect the final result. No one seemed to know the answer. Finally, a great aunt explained to the young girl that when the recipe was first written, a tenderloin roast was too long for her grandmother's regular baking dish; therefore, she needed to remove two inches from the roast, so that it would fit in the pan.

This story illustrates that many times we do things mostly out of custom or habit. We do not realize that our 'baking dish', in this case our mind, continues to be the same size over the years since we rarely stop to ask ourselves why we do things the way we do. Otherwise, how else would the Holocaust, the Inquisition, slavery, or the despicable religious and war crimes have ever been allowed to happen? These crimes were hardly questioned during their time, yet even today, the same atrocities continue to occur in different parts of the world. The reason they continue is that many people are afraid to question, even knowing in their hearts that something is wrong; they blindly follow a false leader or cause. We must believe in ourselves. We must not be afraid to question and raise our voices when the time calls for it. We should not hesitate to give our opinions and question what doesn't make sense to us, not aggressively but assertively and with determination. We avoid stepping out of our comfort zone and avoid conflict to be accepted, or because we fear to be wrong or shamed. At other times, we keep silent and avoid debates because we fear rejection, allowing all sorts of unthinkable injustice.

Many writers suffer from impostor syndrome, thinking everything has been said before, that we have nothing important to say and can't make a difference. However, the most significant movements in the world began with a single person that questioned a belief. Think of Jesus, Gandhi, Abraham Lincoln, or Martin Luther King. A simple woman, Rosa Parks changed history by risking everything the day she refused to relinquish a seat in a bus reserved exclusively for whites, challenging the racist customs of the times. She did not fight, she just took her rightful place. Margaret Mead said it well: 'Never doubt that a small group of thoughtful, committed citizens can change the world. Indeed, it is the only thing that ever has.' We don't need to fight; we just need to take our rightful seat.

Who do you 'think' you are?

One of the most valuable lessons that I have learned comes from the East: you have a mind, and the mind has thoughts, but you are not your thoughts. A mind in harmony with God's consciousness is a limitless mind, a great instrument by which you may discern, obtain information, and create beautiful things. It is important to remember that you are not always the one speaking inside your mind. The mind has thoughts, but your true Self is the observer. Your soul is the authentic Self, the faithful witness, and in essence, the undisturbed part of you that is closest to God.

A mind that never stops chatting, giving its opinions and judgments, and in many instances making you doubt yourself, becomes what Saint Teresa of Ávila called 'the crazy woman of the house'. This voice is the eternal commentator, forever opinionated about your life and that of others. The mind has an archive of everything that happens to you and uses the information as a personal GPS to alert you to previous mistakes, announcing any perceived danger. The job of the mind is to ensure your survival, to keep you safe and protect you from pain. Nevertheless, paralyzing your life might not always be in your best interest unless you are standing at the edge of a cliff.

The soul, together with God, creates unlimited choices, whereas the mind repeats patterns. We 'fall asleep' every time we allow the mind to take over our personality through its automatic programs. Instead of making conscious choices, we begin to react. Enlightenment means to know the difference between being awake or asleep. Being awake is to remember that your true being is forever observing from a never-changing standpoint through the windows of time. Contrary to popular belief, you do not have total control over the thoughts that enter your mind. You can only be aware of them. The secret of alertness is to be able to stop and observe the thoughts before making a choice based on them. Thoughts may come into the mind without an invitation, but only you can decide if you want to become their host.

Plato used analogies comparing the mind to pigeons. If

you find yourself at a park feeding the pigeons, they will fly to you uninvited and even land on your shoulder. If you ignore them and don't feed them, they will eventually leave. However, if you continue to feed them, they will stay, and many others like them will hover over you. The same thing happens with your thoughts: if you feed the negative thoughts of the mind, similar ideas will flock to you in a frenzy. In contrast, if you choose to ignore them and not feed them, they will eventually cease to bother you and go away. In various moments of the day, observe yourself for a minute. What are the thoughts that you continuously dwell on? Where is your focus? What topics are you paying attention to? Our minds make specific distinctions based on beliefs and individual interests at the time. For example, a pregnant woman will notice other pregnant women everywhere, and she will see babies and everything having to do with birthing and labor. An architect will notice all the architectural details in the buildings, and a hairstylist will likewise see hairstyles and color, a fashion designer will look at clothes, and so forth.

Everyone has constant mental conversations; this is what creates your life. Some will worry about the lack of money, while others concentrate on making it. Many will devote their thoughts to politics and others to the entertainment world. In this manner, there will be those concentrating all of their energies on sexuality, while others will focus on other people's faults. Some people even compare themselves to their neighbors to punish themselves for their failures or to boast about their success. A constant and repetitive thought, together with intense emotion, is the silent recipe for creating the future.

The reality we perceive today may be the result of the forgotten thoughts that were rehearsed in our minds yesterday.

Those habitual thoughts are silent words that precede creation, whether you are aware of them or not; however, you are not responsible for every calamity around you. It is a spiritual myth that you are the absolute creator of everything – it is not always your fault when something you feared happens. As human beings, we can also foresee some events. A casual thought won't necessarily become a reality. Thinking of an elephant won't cause one to materialize in your living room. Nonetheless, you can make anything real in your mind by the thoughts you continue to have, even the subconscious ones. When you think of something even when it is not happening, it is awakening all the sensations, mental connections and, personal alarms, just as if they were real. The mind creates reality through the thoughts it believes to be true, particularly those we continually rehearse inside the mind, together with intense emotion. The only points of reference for the mind are in the past or the future. A thought creates a feeling, and a feeling creates either action or non-action; therefore, ask yourself, what kind of thoughts attract your attention most of the time?

Knowing which thought you think of repeatedly will give you information about your beliefs and what's important to you. The awareness will also give you a map to see your future possibilities. Faith can work either way: we can have faith in the best outcome, or we can have faith in the worst outcome. Therefore, we must be careful with this delicate formula to avoid unwanted self-fulfilling prophecies. We are not only observers in this world but participants as well. As quantum mechanics has already discovered, the behavior of a particle of light changes according to the observer.

Be diligent and resolve to observe the thoughts you are generating. This practice will reveal which ideas are holding your attention. Once you identify a thought pattern, only keep those that are genuinely in your best interest. Resolve a recurring issue if you must and let go of the negative ones.

Here are some questions you might ask yourself to identify your thoughts:

- Do you look for the positive qualities in others?
- Are you constantly focusing on your own mistakes as well as those of others?
- Do you continually value others based on their material possessions, or do you notice their subtler qualities?
- Do you frequently dwell on and talk about catastrophes and problems, or do you think about higher solutions for our planet?

Answering the questions above will give you excellent information about the condition of your thought process and its state of consciousness. According to Ignatian spirituality[5], there are two states of consciousness. We

---

[5] Ignatian spirituality, is a system based on the experiences of 16th century theologian Ignatius of Loyola, founder of the Jesuit Order. They are a series of spiritual exercises to help discern God's Will.

are either at peace or in inner turmoil. Ignatius of Loyola calls the two states of being consolation or desolation. Consolation doesn't mean being calmed by exterior pleasures or entertainment, and desolation can happen even when surrounded by loved ones. It is not about eliminating thoughts; it is about learning to discern them. Researchers estimate that we have some sixty thousand thoughts a day and that these thoughts are persistent, repetitive, and mostly negative; worse yet, they are mostly unconscious.

How do you know you're harboring a subconscious negative thought? The way you feel can be used as a compass. When you can't determine the reason for your uneasiness, negative thinking might be to blame. Ask yourself: Am I in a state of consolation or a state of desolation?

People who habitually have a negative attitude will attract thoughts that are just as negative. Likewise, if we are positive, we will attract mostly positive thoughts. Nevertheless, even if you are a positive person, you will inevitably receive disempowering and negative thoughts at times. We live immersed in a pool of thoughts, and most are not even ours. The secret is to remember that you have the power to either entertain a negative thought or let it go completely.

PRACTICE: HOW TO STOP A NEGATIVE THOUGHT

Dada, my beloved teacher from India, used to say that 'a negative thought is like a flame of fire in your hand; the longer you keep it, the more it will burn you.' Pain has a purpose. The moment you realize the flame is burning you, you have the option to remove your hand in time so that the fire will not harm you anymore. In this same manner, you have the alternative to look at a negative thought closely and escort it until it exits through the door of your mind. Simply, let it go. If you resist the thought, you will only make it more persistent. The only way to counteract a negative thought is to accept it – without fighting or resisting – and then by observing it from a place of neutrality, until it finally dissipates.

The saying that *everything happens for a reason* is true; everything that takes place in our line of perception teaches us about our state of mind. Every person you know, even the ones you meet today, every experience that takes place in your environment, and every event you witness all have a message. Nothing is coincidental. Be alert, everything that you can perceive around you happens for your own learning experience.

> *You yourself called the emissaries who knock at your door, and you don't even realize it.*[6]
>
> — Al-Mutamar-Ibn Al Farsi

You are not your story

Experiencing sadness is a normal part of grieving after significant trauma or loss. It is also valid to share your feelings and emotions as part of a healthy recovery process. However, it is not healthy to define yourself permanently with your story. For example, when we hear 'There goes

[6] Found in *Los Emisarios*, a collection of poems by Alvaro Mutis, a Sufi poet from Cordoba 1118–1196

Mrs. Smith, whose husband left her for another woman'; or 'Here comes Mrs. Roberts, a widower for the last twenty years'; or 'Mr. Williams, whose enterprise went bankrupt during the crisis.' These descriptions are the result of the constant telling and retelling of the story to anyone who will listen. When you identify with your story, you attract the possibility of making it real once more, even if only in your mind.

Sadness and suffering are not synonyms. Grief is the natural consequence of any loss, while suffering is the result of not accepting, not yielding, and not forgiving. We suffer because of our need to control a specific undesired outcome, refusing to allow the natural flow of events. The unwanted event becomes like a scar that keeps us playing the past in a loop, like a broken record. When we are in the present – the here and now, without resistance – we do not suffer. The cause of suffering is never the event, but the interpretation of the story. We lose perspective when the facts become contaminated with feelings of frustration, blame, and resentment.

It is inevitable to experience feelings of sadness and loneliness when we lose a dear one, and grieving has a natural process we cannot accelerate. However, to continue to grieve eternally reveals we are unwilling to accept that it was time for our friend or relative to return home. Everything in life passes: shame, sadness, happiness, and life itself. Inevitably life continues its course, and any attempt to manipulate or control it proves to be futile. We cannot change the past, but we can change the story we tell ourselves about the past.

PRACTICE: HOW TO BREAK A NEGATIVE CYCLE

A streak of bad luck begins with your negative thoughts feeding on themselves. One thought alone can raise you to the gates of Heaven, creating a world of beauty and happiness. In the same manner, an obsessive and repetitive thought can plunge you into the depths of hell, creating a miserable life. As I explained earlier, most thoughts are unconscious, meaning you are not aware of them. Unless you make a conscious choice to pause and observe them, they can pass as an unexplained uneasiness in your body.

To know if your thoughts are indeed harmful, simply stop and take a quiet moment to pay attention to what you are feeling and where. Emotions are energy-in-motion, and a 'negative feeling' is our alarm system. 'Scan' your body if you are feeling fear, pain, resentment, or frustration. If you feel restless, this suggests a possible negative thought bringing up uneasy feelings in your body. Usually, our suffering is not about what happened; it is a consequence of our perception of what happened.

First step: Realization

Several times a day, take a moment to scan your whole being. Ask yourself how you are feeling, and where. Then you may say to yourself: 'I am feeling anger, discomfort, and uneasiness, and I feel it in my stomach.' Observe your thoughts and identify what they are saying to you. You can replace any negative thinking by substituting it with an affirmation, either mentally or aloud. If you are thinking, 'Due to the crisis, my business is going under,' there is a possibility that you will feel fear and perhaps pressure in your chest. First, allow yourself to experience the fear; you don't need to be afraid of fear. Validate your feeling; it could be a call for caution. Maybe you need more information to be prepared for an impending change. Whatever the reason, we can overcome fear by taking purposeful action. Simply observe and feel the fear without resistance. Remember that you are not the one who thinks or feels; you are the one who is aware of the thoughts and feelings. Feelings and ideas can change, while your inner Self remains unchangeable, no matter the outside circumstances.

Second step: Will

Gently replace the negative thought with a positive one and state out loud: 'I am naturally prosperous. What I need always reaches me in miraculous ways.' If you don't feel better immediately, don't feel disappointed. Thought-forms do not become automatic overnight, and sometimes they can take some time to be eliminated. Be patient, and simply let things flow. Stay firm in your will and replace the persistent negative thought with an abundant one.

Third step: Conscious action

Stay present in the now, look at the tasks you have before you, and take small actions with love and gratitude; this is all that matters in the end. Mindful action and movement neutralize negative thinking at once. Tasks as simple as ironing or doing the dishes can turn into actual meditation sessions when performed with dignity, presence, and purpose. I just read of a high-profile CEO who washes his dishes every night as a matter of relaxation.

Most of the time, we don't realize that we feel bad. We simply think that this negative state of mind is normal, and we become used to it, creating a habit. Sometimes without noticing, we go about our day frowning, looking sad, angry, or with a frozen face. The most probable cause is a negative thought, which may cause as much pain to yourself as an outside verbal attack or aggression. Often our worst enemy is inside of our heads. We love ourselves by paying attention to the quality of our thoughts, words, and actions.

Traumatic experiences can affect our minds, such as a recent loss, chemical or hormonal imbalances, and other disorders. Do not blame yourself – feelings of hopelessness are not your fault. If, at any point, you feel that negative thoughts are overwhelming you and disrupting your normal life, don't hesitate to ask for professional help.

Finding your balance

There are many techniques for positive thinking that do not consider the rhythms and cycles of life. Some people expect to live in a constant state of ecstasy, such as having a business that only produces profits, living a life of never-ending excitement, or having a love relationship with everlasting passion. When life does not happen the way they expect it, they believe it to be a failure. However, this is a lie since nature does not work in this manner. A plant cannot bear fruit eternally, nor can we make a rose blossom at will when it is not her time. If we could, perhaps we wouldn't appreciate the flowers. We can always experience joy by accepting the natural changes in life, by forgiving ourselves, and being at peace regardless of the time and season, since everything in this world is continually changing. Happy and fortunate times will also pass. They leave the way for new moments and experiences. It is good to relive good memories at times. However, if your attention is fixed exclusively on the good old days, you are going to miss the present while looking at the faded glories and triumphs of the past. The present time is the total sum of all the moments lived – including the good and the not so positive experiences. Sometimes we don't realize that the ordinary present moments are the 'good old times' of tomorrow. Regardless of the undesirable situation you might be experiencing at any particular moment, be completely assured that it too will pass.

Winter doesn't need to last forever. If you remain frozen in your past without flexibility or changes, you'll surely miss all the flowers during spring.

Even if we could be as strong and stable as trees, we will still have cycles in which everything will seem to fall apart. The cold wind does not make the leaves fall in autumn; the trees do this themselves to save energy. In moments of difficulty and despair, we can also find ways to simplify our lives by shedding our attachments, making space for the new. A tree doesn't suffer or complain about losing its leaves. At its core, it knows that losing what is no longer useful is necessary to survive and to receive the new leaves. There are neither negative nor positive times. Winter is not negative; it is just a moment that comes and goes, sheltered by the law of rhythms.

Happiness: A strange and temporary state that only happens when things follow the way you want them to go.

Frustration: A frequent and persistent state you feel when you do not accept the fact that things don't always go your way.

Fulfillment: A natural and permanent state you enjoy when you simply accept what is.

> *Inner peace is to be calm in the middle of the storm; it is to be undisturbed by external conditions. It is to live in total certainty that God is always in control no matter what the outcome and appearances. Inner peace can only be achieved by a personal connection with the Divine.*

You are not your emotions

Emotions are our compass. They show us a conflict between our beliefs and our hearts regarding an important issue in our lives. Emotions are beneficial, they can bring you to a timely reflection, and at other times, they can lead you to necessary action. We don't need to identify ourselves with every emotion we experience since, like the clouds, they are forever passing. Emotions are part of our earthly diving gear, designed for our survival. Through feelings and sensations, they show us where we stand relative to our beliefs. For example, if your core belief is that 'there's not enough', fear or anger will alarm you every time you encounter a perceived threat to your finances or security. Even something as simple as a small rise in the gas price could send a person with a 'there's not enough' belief on a raging episode. A belief is a conclusion you reached after an intense experience or suggestion. A thought that we repeat long enough can also become recorded into a permanent impression, like a mantra. For example, 'Money doesn't grow on trees.'

~

We always assume that feelings are accurate; however, be aware that emotions are not always guided by intuition. Fear or belief can also affect our moods. If not tested with your reason and your soul, a strong emotion may lead to bad choices. Untested enthusiasm can lead to a bad business deal, or even to agree to commitments you don't want to take on. An uncontrolled emotion can destroy a friendship and can also harm yourself or others. A desperate decision taken under a passing emotion – that would have dissipated by morning – can create an unfortunate situation. Emotions will pass, but some actions are not reversible. For this reason, be it fear or enthusiasm, it is advisable to delay any decision until one is clear of the intense emotion, unless, of course, there is an emergency.

My teacher Dada used to say that we should be careful with the words we use when feeling a strong emotion since spoken words are irreversible. Just like a tube of toothpaste, once you press the contents out, they can't be pushed back in. Nevertheless, we must allow ourselves to feel our emotions in a healthy way, without judging, denying, or evading them. All emotions need to be experienced fully but responsibly by allowing yourself to feel tears, laughter, or anger. The only way to let an emotion out of your system is by experiencing it fully. Repressed emotions hiding somewhere in our bodies may turn out to cause trouble in the future, bursting when we least expect it. It is also essential that from an early age, we allow children to express their emotions safely and in a healthy way, since avoiding tears or anger will eventually bring negative consequences. A stronger person is not necessarily the one who doesn't cry.

Have you ever noticed how natural it is for children to process their emotions? Just moments after living through an intense tantrum, screams, and all, they can drop that emotion and continue laughing as if nothing had happened. On the other hand, parents as good adults can stay immersed in their own 'tantrums' for hours, sometimes even for years! Children have a natural ability to process emotions without resistance or judgment. They know how to look at the present with new eyes and without resentment. Changing how to carry yourself can affect your emotions and vice versa. The secret is to be alert and to practice a more positive way of being for your own benefit. Today choose new thoughts and practice by rehearsing joy with a big smile and walking tall, with your head held high. Act in this manner, and your emotions will eventually follow your body's lead.

PRACTICE: WHAT TO AVOID WHEN FEELING A STRONG EMOTION

Whenever you feel a strong emotion surging, such as an angry outburst, imagine that you are intoxicated and unable to drive, and therefore, unable to make the right decisions. Since you can become 'drunk' with anger, wait until the morning after the strong emotion when you can use your intellect to put things in perspective. Before making a decision, *have a coffee with God*. Out-of-control emotions will remove all objectivity and keep you from seeing things as they are, making you behave in unsuitable ways. Feelings come and go. If you watch them without judgment and experience them fully, they will eventually vanish. Otherwise, they will control your life.

It is essential to remember that emotions are messengers that warn you when there is a conflict between your mind, heart, and soul. These emotions require your full attention so that you may respond accordingly.

THE YOGI AND THE EMPEROR

This is a story I heard many times from my dear teacher Dada:

Emperor Alexander the Great, while traveling in India, searched for a wise yogi to bring back to Greece with him. When he found a yogi praying in the forest, the emperor demanded with all his authority: 'Come with me to Greece!'

The yogi continued with his prayers and did not budge at all. Seeing that the wise man showed no sign of interest or obedience, Alexander felt an uncontrollable rage. It was the first time anyone had dared ignore, question, or reject his orders.

He drew his sword and threatened the yogi with death, shouting, 'Don't you know I can behead you for not obeying my orders?' Annoyed, he continued, 'I am Alexander the Great, the emperor and conqueror of the world!'

The yogi replied with the calm attitude of wisdom that he always had. 'You claim to be the conqueror of the world, but I think that you are just a slave to my slave.'

'How can that be?' asked an enraged Alexander, baffled by such a reply.

The yogi then explained, 'I have mastered anger. Anger is my slave. You have just lost your control to anger. Right here and now, you have become a slave to my slave, meaning a slave to anger.'

Remember that everything you think, feel, or experience is transitory, like fog in a valley. The valley may experience fog, rain, or wind, yet it is not any of those climate conditions. Likewise, you may have to live through tears, rage, and pain, yet you are none of those sensations. Do not identify yourself with darkness. Allow the light of the sun to shine over you. After the bad weather has passed, you will soon see how the valley will continue being a valley, and you will continue being you.

We are all a work in progress; however, some people are eternally postponing life because they are forever 'working on themselves'. Resolving your inner conflicts is not about 'cleaning' past emotions all the time. It is not healthy to open up the garbage disposal every second. Observe yourself; however, know that continually digging up your past can contaminate your present when done indiscriminately. There is a time and a process for everything. Don't wait to live the life you deserve until you 'deal with all of your stuff'. Seek help if you must if you feel that you cannot handle your own thoughts, emotions, or body. If you see yourself reacting uncontrollably or are entertaining thoughts of not wanting to live any longer, get professional help immediately. Physical conditions can make it hard to deal with emotions – a chemical imbalance, a sugar problem, and allergies to some foods, even an unchecked thyroid can affect how we heal. Make an effort to find the root of the problem, with a genuine commitment to let go of the past while creating a new future.

PRACTICE: REVERSING A WRONG BELIEF

To heal from a negative emotion, make an effort to identify the cause. To change the belief and the thought that causes pain, you will often need to address the behavior that is causing the conflict. Only false beliefs can prevent you from seeing the truth. Here I share some common ones.

- **I am not good enough.** If you are suffering because you are in an abusive relationship, first try to identify the belief; for example, 'I am not good enough.' Then, to resolve the emotion, you will also need to change the action. In this case, it would be asking for help or ending a relationship, since this relationship (action) conflicts with your integrity and with what your soul knows to be your highest good. The inner conversation about this situation will hold you hostage saying falsely, 'This is all my fault,' or 'You are not worthy enough to deserve an honest, loving romantic relationship.' As long as you continue in that relationship (the action), guilt (the emotion) will continue to warn you of the fact that you are not living in integrity with your Self (your soul). All the emotion processing will serve no purpose until you don't resolve the conflict. The emotion will repeat itself until you are safe. In this case, the emotion is not only a red flag but also a blessing. Emotions are your best warning system.

- **I cannot live alone.** In this situation, you would probably act possessively towards your partner (the action) and experience fear of losing this person (the emotion). You will see danger every time the partner innocently looks the other way. Unless you change this belief (realize that your happiness does not depend on other people) and recognize that you cannot control others (new belief), you will continue to be jealous, possessive, and eternally fearful of a loss: a perfect formula for suffering. If you choose to change your beliefs, and you choose well, you will enjoy the relationship free of attachment.
- **There's not enough.** In the case where you are constantly afraid of losing your money (fear is the emotion), you can change the belief – 'There isn't enough,' 'I'm not worth it,' 'I can't,' 'There's a crisis' – with a new way of seeing things – 'The world is abundant,' 'I am worthy,' 'I have a purpose,' 'God is my abundance.' Otherwise, all of your actions will be subconsciously contaminated by fear, which will always define the choices you make.

The nature of your thoughts and emotions will affect the integrity of your actions and reactions. Some emotions come from unconscious beliefs, with no apparent basis, while others will have a clear origin that you can see. You don't need to identify every emotion to be happy, but it helps to know yourself better. Therapy is an excellent way to help discover hidden beliefs. The important thing is to be able to identify them and to know that emotions come to warn us of a deeper inner conflict.

Vanishing our shadows

We are all born with talents, but we may also have a tendency to develop particular negative emotions. Some call them shadows, but I call them 'design flaws'. We don't know for sure why these flaws exist or where they come from. You may have a propensity for negative emotion or thought. These shadows sometimes walk beside us throughout our lifetime, but these shadows are not real. You probably are familiar with one or two. A particular emotional disposition to a false thought and the button that causes us to flare up in pain when pushed by a family member, making us react uncontrollably. For some, it is low self-esteem; for others, the insecurity of never feeling good enough; and for still others, it is loneliness even if living with someone else. The common denominator is fear.

These thoughts are disguised as friends, constantly whispering in our ears. The key to overcoming them is to become aware of them while not engaging with their story. You must remember that they are just shadows. When you choose to surrender to God, seeing them through the light of your connection with Him, all their power disappears. Even if they come back, you can automatically cancel any control they might have over you with the power of awareness.

The light of love will always dispel the shadow of fear.

Many techniques work to clear subconscious emotions from the past. In the following exercise, I describe one that I have found very useful.

PRACTICE: HOW TO PROCESS A STRONG EMOTION

The key to processing an emotion which arises on the spur of the moment, or that you have felt recently, is by allowing yourself to experience it completely. One way is to express it either mentally or verbally. You may also write about it in a journal. Express your thoughts and feelings; in other words, observe your mind, identify its beliefs, and fully experience the feelings of that emotion in your body. Let them be; trying to control will only empower the emotion.

For example: If your partner has broken up your relationship, practice this new way of seeing that you are not your emotions, nor your mind nor your body; you are only the observer who is experiencing these sensations. This is important distinction.

1. **Mind:** Instead of saying to yourself, 'I am not good enough for him,' make an effort to stop and observe yourself from the witness point of view. This when you watch yourself and your thoughts. Now you may replace the above thought with: 'I am not that thought. I am only experiencing this mistaken passing thought that I am not good enough, and that I don't consider myself attractive as I am, either for my partner or even for myself.' Awakening is rebuking the harmful lie with the opposite. 'I am beautiful. I am worthy and a wonderfully-made child of God.'
2. **Emotion:** Instead of saying to yourself, 'I am sad,' make an effort to stop and observe yourself from the witness point of view. This is when you watch yourself and your

emotions. Now you may replace the above thought with: 'I am not that emotion. I am only experiencing this passing hurtful feeling through the emotion of sadness.'

3. **Body**: Instead of saying to yourself, 'I am sick,' make an effort to stop and observe yourself from the witness point of view as if you were watching yourself. Now you may replace the above thought with: 'I am not this sickness. I am only experiencing in my body this passing experience of feeling unwell.'

Another example might be if someone has betrayed you in business. First, feel the negative emotion fully, without blocking it, and immediately imagine yourself surrounded by a bright light, one of love and peace. Bless the situation, accept it without judgment and be grateful, not for what happened, but for the lessons learned, for you will only be able to heal if you accept and learn from what cannot be undone. We can always choose to make diamonds out of the carbon rocks that life throws at us. Everything that happens is part of the curriculum for our personal learning. Call upon the Will of God, so that He may heal this situation. Change your life's direction. Christianity borrows the Greek word 'metanoia' to describe a change of heart and mind. Allow the Divine plan to guide your intuition towards the tools you will need for healing, for example, a book, a sign in nature, a message or a new insight about the situation. Allow the situation to unfold naturally, without pushing or upsetting yourself. All things pass, and everything has its reason for being.

The secret to attaining mastery over your emotions is to be able to discern truth from falsehood. Know that emotions are involuntary and simply allow yourself to experience them from a level of awareness, paying attention to the message they bring you, and then just letting them go.

Flexibility

Flexibility is the logical answer when any undesired change challenges us. Flexibility means looking at a new situation and responding accordingly: Was the flight canceled? Was the house you wanted sold? Is your relationship over? Don't blame anyone. Don't resist it. Don't regret it. Just practice acceptance and be patient; this is not the same as resignation. Accept the fact that things don't always turn out the way you expect. Be assured that in the end, all things will work themselves out for the better.

Lack of flexibility can also be the result of old beliefs that we haven't examined. When faced with a change in life, learn from the river. The river doesn't stop when faced with an obstacle. The flow of water doesn't stop with the boulder; it doesn't fight them. The river transcends the rocks by surrounding and embracing them, continuing on its unencumbered journey to the sea.

There is always another way, an alternative path. If you are on the road and come to an unexpected detour with a STOP sign, then pause. There's a reason. Breathe and relax. There is a strong possibility that changing the course might be the best decision for you, even if you can't see what the warning means at that moment. If you choose to continue on the road ignoring the signs, you might find yourself falling down a precipice that was forewarned with that simple STOP sign.

Which is more flexible, a fragile bamboo tree, or a mighty oak? According to a Chinese proverb, the flimsy bamboo (the stronger the wind, the more it bends) is more resistant to hurricane winds than the mighty oak (whose rigidity makes it break). Real power is not a matter of strength but flexibility.

How to overcome suffering

Responsibility is the beginning of peace. Being responsible does not mean that you are to blame for everything that happens. For example, you don't control the moon or the sun, or the choices others make. Being responsible, when you are healthy, is the ability to choose and *respond* to any event. The key to ending suffering is to let go of your attachment to the outcome of any situation and to surrender into God's hands and Will. The true secret to freedom is to say, 'I only desire what God wants for me.' Have preferences in place of desires, and accept the present and what is. Only from this place of acceptance can actual change come about.

When the Dalai Lama was asked how he dealt with regrets from the past. He was asked whether he got rid of them. After giving it some thought the Dalai Lama answered, 'I didn't get rid of it. It still there. But ... it isn't associated with a feeling of heaviness or a quality pulling back.'[7] He continues to explain that it would not be helpful to anyone to let that feeling be a source of discouragement and depression, without purpose. He teaches that we

---

[7] Dalai Lama and Howard C. Cutler, in *The Art of Happiness: A Handbook for Living*, (New York: Riverhead Books, 2020), p. 160.

should not be attached to our past. We need to learn to stop reliving, reviewing, and exaggerating it continuously, and instead let the past take care of itself.

The power of accountability is to address the needs of the present moment, including taking all the necessary steps to avoid repeating past errors. Overcoming suffering happens when we stop resisting our experiences and what is. Acceptance is a death blow to the ego.

> *God, grant me the serenity to accept the things I cannot change, the courage to change the things I can, and the wisdom to know the difference.*
>
> — Reinhold Niebuhr

2

YOUR INNER PRESENCE

THE INNER PRESENCE REFERS TO OUR 'PRE-ESSENCE', THE essence of the soul that was there before us and lives beyond time. To be filled with this pre-essence is to live fully in the now. A person filled with the fragrance of Inner Presence is charismatic, attracting others without any effort. Nature is the best teacher of Inner Presence, flowers and birds are unassuming, not wishing they were something different – unworried, unhurried. It is the result of being in the present.

On the other hand, not being in the present is one of the most common causes of accidents, communication problems, family disagreements, mistakes at work, and misunderstandings. To be present is to be aware, conscious, and awake. Enlightenment is the ability to know who you are and who others are as well.

Life is not a rehearsal, as English novelist Rose Tremain says. Most of us are not in the present; instead, we live life as a rehearsal, a lifelong preparation for that perfect day we have pictured in our minds. We live for tomorrow, confabulating an ideal imaginary day we believe only exists somewhere in the future. We even save our best attire and tableware for a 'special occasion'. In the meantime, we miss out on what is happening right before our eyes: the only moment that is real.

We sit at the dinner table of life, and instead of eating the meal served right in front of us, we prefer to savor the pictures on the menu with our minds. The antidote for this unconscious state of mind is to live enjoying the here and now with all of our senses – to fully experience the present, regardless of how extraordinary, terrible or monotonous it may appear. Being here – now – is living without trying to change the present, without judging ourselves or others, without making comparisons with better times, expecting the worst, or trying to control outcomes by calculating our actions.

We are mentally 'asleep' when time slips through our hands without leaving a trace in our consciousness. We travel from point A to point B only to realize we have no recollection of how or why we arrived there. A similar situation happens when we reach the end of the day and have no idea what happened at breakfast. Perhaps, instead of enjoying a cup of coffee or listening to our son's school story, we were too busy looking at the seemingly perfect lives of others in social media. In the same manner, one day, we find we are turning forty-five and realize that we never really stopped to question: Where are we heading in life? We mistakenly believed we had all the time in the world, only to find, a little too late, that the child you did not listen to at breakfast has become a young adult and is ready to leave for college. Another wake-up call happens when we realize that our inner child has also grown up, but without fulfilling his own dreams and purpose. Then we wonder: How did I get to this point in life? What has happened in the meantime?

In the later part of our journey, we also realize that we missed the stop where our dreams were waiting for us. Most likely, it was fear that crushed those dreams that we never even explored because we were worried about imaginary events that never came to pass. Some dreams didn't come to fruition because we changed our minds, but others were lost because we were paralyzed by fear and self-doubt.

In the journey of our lives, we also missed the view. Because instead of enjoying the scenery, we got distracted by the past in the rear mirror. Sooner or later, we all must come face to face with the fact that no one can reverse time.

The good news is that it is never too late to awaken to our present, and every moment is a new opportunity to begin anew. Today you can choose to make peace with yourself. Let go of what never was and start living what is now. Don't leave your life at the mercy of the wind. Take back the driver's seat of your life; it is never too late to live in the present.

We can be the architects and creators of our own lives. There is a time for everything, as Ecclesiastes would say: *a time to dream and imagine, a time to draw the blueprint plans, a time to plan and coordinate, a time to build and a time to admire what was created*. Still, life is what happens while we are searching for our dreams. The most important and elusive moment in time is called *the meantime*.

All is good. There is nothing you lack. Dissatisfaction is an invention of the ego, and on a positive note, it is also a device designed so that we may continue growing. What is it like to live from the perspective of your Inner Presence? Contentment is our natural state at birth and old age – when physical energy has diminished and it's time to leave behind the season of doing and planning, for the season of being and living. In old age, we naturally return to that Inner Presence, and the cycle of life is completed. Inner Presence is evidenced by the freedom from thought.

People today consider their daily struggles as their normal state of consciousness when, in reality, it is an altered state of consciousness. The worry, the anxiety, and the stress we are so used to is an artificial state of being. Our natural state is Inner Presence and enjoying the inner peace it brings. Interestingly enough, when we experience these fleeting sparks of Inner Presence, peace, and light, we mistakenly think that we have reached a higher state foreign to us. Who hasn't had one of those unforgettable moments of oneness and awe while walking in nature? The truth is the other way around. This peaceful state of consciousness is the natural state, and we should be enjoying it daily. To be able to see the Inner Presence in another begins by being present ourselves in total authenticity.

Presence is to be in God's Presence, witnessing everything with devotion and as a part of God, including yourself. Know that if we allow it, God can express His love through us. Faith is knowing that God always works on the side of your highest good. To be present is to become embodied with your spirit, filled with life, curiosity, and vibrancy.

Your eyes will have a special light. Presence is energy. When not present or aware, you look empty and absent, as if there were 'nobody home'. Our world seems to be filled with people who are asleep, much like robots and zombies.

Living in the Presence is feeling sensations in your limbs while simultaneously attending the task in front of you. It is learning to live fully in the present moment, without losing the awareness of yourself.

PRACTICE: BEING AWAKE

Take a moment by yourself several times during the day and breathe deeply. Exhale with a long ah, letting all the tension go. Continue by activating your five senses. How do your surroundings smell? What colors do you see? How are your hands feeling? Are you cold? Can you feel your toes? That's it. It is that simple. A hundred percent Inner Presence, guaranteed!

Living under the Presence of God is to know that He has your back. We just need to rest and allow all of His power and goodness to protect us at each moment.

Nature is your best teacher for learning to be in the present moment. Listen to the sounds of the waves, see the birds in flight, smell the perfume of the flowers, taste the spices, and feel the earth.

To commune with nature is the best way to reach the state of Inner Presence. Being present is to be available and entirely in touch with everything that surrounds you.

THE GREATEST TREASURE IN THE WORLD: A RIDDLE

Beginning today, you may choose to enjoy every moment of your existence, not allowing one more second to slip away from your life. You can open your eyes and live this apparently ordinary and imperfect moment, yet this is where the greatest of treasures are found. This treasure is irreplaceable, unique, original, more precious than all of the diamonds in the world. As priceless as life itself, one-of-a-kind. It gives no guarantees and is always surprising; this treasure is indiscernible, because it is simple and can be monotonous, uncelebrated, almost unnoticeable.

You cannot buy it even if you have all the gold in the world, and even though it is eternal, if you were to lose it, it would never return. If you try to capture it, the treasure will only slip through your fingers. It is the enemy of time, but a friend of eternity. It is the enemy of those who are asleep, but a friend of those who are awake. The treasure sometimes comes disguised as fatigue, boredom, or disgust. Other times it is hiding in the flutter of a butterfly, in the smile of a child. Within the sweetness of a mango and the bitterness of a goodbye, behind a warm summer breeze and the sound of showers over the tin ceiling; between the cooing of a newborn and the regrets of the aged, between the echo of laughter and the solitude of a single tear.

This treasure is unrivaled among all the gifts God has given you, yet it is hidden in an unlikely place. It rests in your hands momentarily like a passing dove, but like water, it slips through your fingers never to return. Once it departs, it can never be replaced.

Sometimes it is longed for; sometimes it is forgotten. The grandest of all treasures, the most valuable possession in the whole world, yet few recognize it, and even fewer can appreciate it the moment they have it.

This treasure is ... the Now.

Conclusion

If I am neither my body nor my thoughts, nor the voice speaking in my mind, nor my emotions nor my beliefs, then who am I, really?

You are the one observing, the one listening, a piece of God, and an infinite being who is timeless and ageless. When you watch a thought, your soul's awareness shines through your eyes like beams of light, diffusing all negativity just as the sun disperses the fog. This state does not mean you are free of negative thoughts; it indicates you are at peace despite being aware of them. Negative or positive events and situations will take root inside your thoughts, depending on the seeds that you have planted. You now have the power to plant a new seed of love for your future, which will grow assisted by your will and intention. You must believe in this possibility and have unbreakable faith in the possibility of a new life. Simply stating aloud, 'I am willing' will suffice for God. He will then help you see things differently, casting His light over all areas of your life.

You are not alone; God is always with you.

— Dada J.P. Vaswani

... And also, with me.

PART II

WHERE AM I HEADED?

THE SEVEN AREAS OF YOUR LIFE

Before knowing where you are headed, it would be convenient to ask: Where are you standing? You may have the exact address of the place you want to go, yet if you don't know where you are standing in reference to that place, even the most sophisticated map in the world will be of little use.

In the following pages, we will examine your personal portfolio, divided into seven specific areas of life. The first step for any significant change is to be able to see and accept your current reality, whatever it may be – since you cannot change what you cannot see. Once you have completed this step, you will be able to create a new vision and a new reality with the tools provided in this book. No great effort is required. Just read calmly through these pages. Live in the present and observe yourself. That is all you need to do for now.

Your personal portfolio and the wheel of life

The idea of a portfolio came to me during a meeting I had with a financial advisor. As I sat in his office, he showed me a PowerPoint image of a circle divided into several triangles of different colors. Since it was close to lunchtime, I couldn't help but compare it to a sliced pizza.

He advised me on the best way to invest my income for a better yield and assess each area to avoid risks. Later, as I reviewed his advice, I thought about how promising it would be to implement this same theory in our personal lives – assessing each area to ensure we are investing in what is really valuable and truly important to us. It is inconceivable to see how much time we spend in making sure we make a sound purchase or financial investment, yet how much disregard we have towards significant decisions in our personal life. If we do not oversee each area of our lives, if we do not invest in each one and evaluate it consistently, we may end up in spiritual bankruptcy.

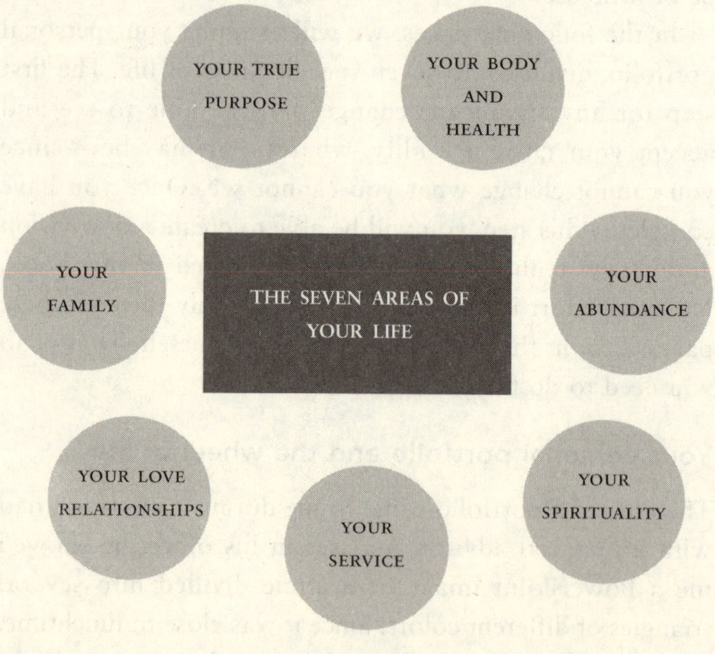

A lack of balance among the different areas of our lives may create chaotic outcomes. Maybe you are spending too much time and effort on your career while neglecting your personal relationships or focusing too much on your finances while overlooking your health. Thanks to the individual portfolio, you will be able to look into each area of your life and decide what changes need to happen to optimize the benefits.

There are no magic formulas. The effort we make in any area will bring a result, and the lack of energy will also bring a consequence.

PRACTICE: REVISITING EVERY AREA OF YOUR LIFE

Take a moment to go through each of the areas of your life shown below. Use your journal or any notebook that you can divide into sections. Make a list of your values in each one of the seven areas of your life in the order of their priority to you at this moment. Be honest; this is not a test of your character; it's an exercise to help you understand your present situation. In the same area, write a second list, next to the first, in the order of the actual effort and time you spend on them. Unsurprisingly, you will find that you have better results in the areas where you are more organized. In contrast, there will be deficiencies in the areas that you don't give so much of your attention, even if you believe they are your moral priority. The ideal is to have a balance.

3

YOUR BODY AND HEALTH

WELL-BEING IS OUR NATURAL STATE OF BEING. OUR BODY works as a harmonious symphony. Similar in principle to a power transformer, the body is a channel that conducts God's vital energy. In its optimal state, it allows the life force to flow through unobstructed. When this transformer deteriorates because of our negative thoughts, emotions, attitudes, abuses, or habits, it blocks the natural flow of energy, creating stagnation, which in turn creates disease. As in the world of power and electricity, fluctuations in the flow of voltage will harm the best equipment.

We don't create our illnesses, but we might contribute to the conditions that allow *dis-ease*, which is a revealing word in itself. We don't always have access to the full scope of information to understand the exact reasons behind a particular illness or condition. Many times, a disease is 'the tax on pleasure', as naturalist John Ray brilliantly puts it. Even when an illness is caused by our excesses in food, stress, or worry, we should not feel shame. Everyone acts and responds to the best of their capabilities. Sometimes illness works as an emergency call to bring us back to our original state of well-being and harmony. When challenged by disease, the first step is acceptance. We cannot change what has not been accepted – this is not the same as resignation, which is to give up on life. Second, we need to allow ourselves to feel and express our anger and sadness. Like the stages of grief, we mourn our loss of health, which is frequently taken for granted, mistakenly thinking that vitality will last forever. We need to respond with dignity to illness; in a sense, we need to 'own it' by avoiding feelings of victimhood, shame, beating up ourselves, or blaming God.

We all have a perfect design

God holds our original blueprint in His universal memory, a faultless map that He previously designed. When we become ill, that plan automatically sends a Divine command to restore the body to its original state. The same is true with all of nature and the universe.

If we injure a finger, we immediately disinfect the injury and, at the same time, notice how Divine intelligence heals by regenerating all the tissues to their original order. This self-diagnostic and self-healing system is also known as *spontaneous healing*, as Dr. Andrew Weil notes in his book by the same name. However, if we begin to doubt our ability to heal, or if we continue to poke our wounds and interfere with the healing, the process will be delayed. An excellent medicine is non-resistance; for both the body and the mind would benefit from being relaxed, and thus heal faster.

The art of medicine consists of amusing the patient while nature cures the disease.

— Voltaire

Healing the cause

Frequently, we treat our illnesses through methods that work only on the surface of the problem. True healing is eradicating the cause and healing the soul. Most medications and treatments relieve the symptom only temporarily. We are body, mind, emotions, and spirit, and healing occurs when we care for all these four areas simultaneously. Illness is the name we call a symptom, depending on where it manifests in our body. Most doctors will treat disease by fighting the symptoms, while we should also be working on eradicating the causes. One of the leading underlying causes of illness is stress, which affects our immune system, our first defense against disease.

In other words, your body has the ability to use Divine energy for self-healing. This Divine energy works in total connection with God, asking for healing by His Will and believing and focusing on the desired health outcome. After this invitation, many miracles may happen.

When we ignore its warnings, the body falls into disease

If you fail to put gas in the tank of your car when the warning light comes on, your vehicle will stop at some point inevitably. The body works the same way; if we ignore its signals, the body will eventually stop. After detecting a discrepancy, the mind is the first to warn us by sending thousands of thoughts. When there is a disagreement between your body, mind, and soul, a battle begins. The mind works to find harmony; it receives the information and sends a message to the soul by way of emotions: 'Get ready; something is just not right!' And thus, the healing begins. Unstable emotions and not feeling well, are the warning lights in human beings. Illnesses do not start solely in the physical body. Science has done extensive research about the connection between body, mind, emotions, and disease.

For example, a battered wife living in an internal conflict will have the inner knowledge that she needs to act according to reason, which is instructing her to leave an intolerable situation. In contrast, beliefs learned in her Church, for example, will remind her that marriage is 'till death do us part', and that she must care for her husband above all things. Her mind creates a chain of thoughts that will shift her emotions (in this case) into destructive ones such as guilt, suffering, shame, and anger. If not attended to, these emotions might manifest themselves as a physical symptom. Stress can affect our immune system, creating a weakness in the body. If we do not undo the original causes of these emotions and thoughts, the preexisting vulnerability might become chronic and develop into illnesses.

Illness as teacher

Diseases may be congenital; for example, a physical defect. However, there is always an opportunity to feel at peace amid the worst situation. God does not cause the illness but He always has an unknown plan for healing, for both the affected and those close to Him, including family members. It is important to remember that illnesses are not punishments. There are predispositions and learned ways of living, eating, and responding; however, studies have shown that genetics is not necessarily a determining factor in the development of a disease.[8] A condition in the family is not necessarily a guarantee that it will be inherited. However, an incorrect belief or fear of developing an illness or learned bad habits may affect us. It is also important to realize that disease is not a test of our faith. There are many factors behind the cause of illness, including lifestyle and environmental exposure. Still, if we invite God, He can always use this negative situation to help us grow and develop higher human qualities – like compassion, mercy, and empathy.

> *May your food be your medicine and your medicine be your food.*
>
> — Hippocrates

What would happen if we fed a Ferrari sugar instead of fuel? It would immediately break down. Why then do we keep filling our much more sophisticated bodies with alcohol, drugs, sugar, salt, chemical products, and numerous pollutants? Negative thoughts and the feelings that follow are also toxic 'food'. Everything we feed our senses affects us, including movies, games, and music filled with negative messages – it is vital to feed our body, mind, soul, and spirit with healthy foods and positive visuals, thoughts, and emotions.

---

[8] Stephen M. Rappaport, 'Genetic Factors Are Not the Major Causes of Chronic Diseases,' Plos One 11, no. 4 (2016), https://doi.org/10.1371/journal.pone.0154387.

'Believe the diagnosis, not the prognosis'[9]

Deepak Chopra explains it well. Conventional medicine needs to work together and be in harmony with the main medical fields: spiritual and natural medicine. The cooperation of these practices will allow our bodies and minds to facilitate God's light to work within us and eliminate the root of the disease.

I urge everyone to have regular checkups and, in case of an emergency, visit their allopathic doctors, that is, doctors of conventional medicine. Once the crisis is under control, visit the holistic doctor as well as a therapist, to identify any underlying emotional causes. The ideal is to have these professionals work together.

Do not empower disease

You may heal your life, or better yet, allow God to restore it, but you must actively assist in the process. Remember that you are not the illness; therefore, you must not describe yourself in terms of the disease. Avoid phrases like 'I am addicted to ...' or 'I am depressed ...'

It is not about denying an illness. The first step towards healing is total acceptance; the next one is looking for help. Nevertheless, empowering the disease will not make us better. To overcome any condition, we must redirect the focus of our mind in the opposite state of the undesired health condition in your life, while doing everything possible to avoid the stress factors and triggers that can interfere with healing.

---

[9] Quote by Deepak Chopra.

Be careful when saying 'I AM' because it is a powerful declaration. We can declare health, in the same manner, we can declare disease. Faith works both ways. You can define, create, and perpetuate positive or negative conditions with the words I AM – they will always work regardless of how you use them. It is important not to turn the story of being sick into a way of life. Even though we don't create our illnesses, for some, the disease can become a guarantee to companionship, attention, or unending sympathy. They are the ones that seem to have no interest in getting better. One good question to ask is: What benefit do we believe we are getting by perpetuating a condition? Resisting assistance isn't advisable either. For some who have been too independent, the lesson might be in allowing another person to help.

Healing is about responding to life from a place of power while observing our reactions objectively. You can always choose how you react to what happens, even when you don't have full control over the circumstances or the outcome. We can always choose love over fear and hope over despair. If you place all of your focus on solutions and not on the problems, you will soon recover your health – remember that health is more than a bodily description. A better description of overall health is: well-being.

Even if the body fails to respond, true healing happens when God resides in our hearts permanently healing our soul and giving us unconditional peace, independent of the state of our physical health.

Undoubtedly, attaining inner peace is more important than actual physical health, since peace is what allows you to have the power to face any obstacle with optimism.

Overcoming the fear of death

To live a full life first, you must come to terms with death. To conquer the fear of death, we must learn to see it as an impending process in the natural cycle of physical life, and not a catastrophe.

When we accept death as a natural and unavoidable fact of life, we put an end to its power over us. As we free ourselves from the fear of death, we begin to live each moment with love and gratefulness. The way to conquer the fear of death is by having reverence for life. We can attain this freedom by learning to live in the present.

> *The worst death is to live as if we were already gone, while still breathing.*

People who are not prepared to die are seldom prepared to live. The universal remedy for any illness, negative situation or problem is to live every minute with love and total peace while focusing on the best possible outcome regardless of external conditions.

When Jesus healed, he turned his attention away from sin, and when he resurrected Lazarus, he turned his attention away from death and placed all his faith in the perfection of Heaven. While accepting God's Will, he looked up to Heaven, which is only love and perfection, believing without any doubt that he was being heard. One decisive detail is that Jesus had complete faith that God always listens to our prayers and thanked God before a miracle was granted. He said: 'Father, I thank You that You have heard Me. I knew that You always hear me.'[10] Invoking Divine Will, while leaving the outcome to God, is the true formula for creating a miracle.

A simple way to care for the body

Our body is the temple of the spirit, and as such, we need to take good care of it through sound practices and healthy habits. Energy is the currency in our savings account of life. If we don't use it correctly, it will run out too soon. Our energy is the vital charge that our 'earthly diving gear' needs to perform at peak condition.

There are many ways to recharge and protect our bodies and let go of the accumulated negativity. In the following list, I will share with you my favorite practices.

They are simple ways, based on common sense, to accomplish this recharging:

1. **Going to bed early.** The best sleep and real rest take place between ten at night and four in the morning.
2. **Napping.** Closing your eyes and taking a short nap in the afternoon, or whenever needed.
3. **Dancing.** Dancing frees the soul and increases positive energy.
4. **Listening.** Enjoy classical and inspiring music.
5. **Breathing.** Try deep and conscious breathing. Filling in your lungs and exhaling, emptying them entirely,

[10] John 11:42

is one of the best and most straightforward practices. Also, breathing in from the diaphragm is a technique of deep inhalation that is very different from breathing from the chest. It is the most natural and efficient way to breathe.

6. **Touching.** Receiving a massage or self-massaging.
7. **Meditating.** Practicing silence and meditation daily. True meditation is a process of emptying of the mind, a preparation for God. He will soothe your thoughts, your emotions, and your spirit – a withdrawal from the world. On the other hand, the purposeful repetition of prayers fills your soul with peace, calms your mind, and keeps your energy levels stable. As a result, you will enjoy good health.
   Sleep is the body's way to rest, while silence is the way of the mind.
8. **Making love.** If you are in a loving relationship, making love with your partner is healthy. It releases dopamine and oxytocin, rejuvenating both partners' energies.
9. **Exercising.** Finding the sport or activity that best suits you. Yoga, Tai Chi, Chi Kung, or Qigong are some options. Enjoy swimming or tennis, or just try the practice of walking consciously in nature.
10. **Enjoying nature.** Practice *grounding*. Walking barefoot on a green lawn or in the sand has been known to lower blood viscosity and blood pressure. Sitting in nature, heals. Hug a tree. Breathing in and absorbing the blue of the sky and the green of the trees is healing.
11. **Drinking water.** Water makes the difference between a grape and a raisin. Imagine how it works on our skin!
12. **Swimming.** Swimming in the ocean or taking a salt bath

absorbs toxins. A warm bath infused with previously boiled medicinal herbs cleanses and energizes. Water makes up about 90% of our blood's liquid, 78% of our brain and 65% of our body.

(Check first with your doctor; pregnant women need to be particularly aware of certain oils. Check with your medical provider before starting any new diet or exercise.)

13. **Sunning.** Soaking in the sun at low-intensity hours increases our energy. Remember that sunlight is one of the most critical energy sources, like oxygen and food. It is also a great antidote to depression.
14. **Practicing healthy eating habits.** Try to eat only natural, unprocessed proteins and carbohydrates as much as you can. Eat a rainbow of colors in fruits and vegetables. Limit meat, dairy, sugar, alcohol, and salt consumption. Himalayan salt is a better alternative to the standard white table salt.
15. **Stopping addictions.** We cannot be ourselves if we are slaves of any form of addiction, including nicotine and recreational drugs. Look for help and support, if necessary.

A healthy diet

Human beings can undoubtedly survive in any environment and with a wide variety of foods. Still, our modern lifestyle has pushed us far from what our natural and optimum diet should be. We drink and give our babies milk from other species and eat meat contaminated with chemical products and hormones. A significant number of the ecological and health problems that we are experiencing come from the imbalance we have created with our unrestrained meat consumption. It would be ideal to start taking responsibility for what we eat and also consider, with the help of our doctors, the possibility of supplementing our diets with the minerals and nutrients most processed foods lack.

If you eat meat, make sure it is organic and raised humanely. If it is from cattle, make sure they were fed by grazing or 'grass-fed' as opposed to being fed with hormone and growth-inducing cereals, which end up in our bodies and adversely affect children. These recommendations are also applicable to poultry and dairy products.

The way we feed ourselves will continue to change as our species continues to evolve towards subtler and more compassionate nutrition. Farm-to-table initiatives are growing, and I believe that a mostly plant-based diet will eventually be our ideal form of eating. New research has found that a plant-based or low-meat diet has an impact on health and longevity.[11] However, forcing yourself to be a vegetarian when you are not ready will only make you crave your old diet more out of plain desperation. When you feel prepared to do so, start with gradual changes with the help of your doctor.

I eat mostly plant-based meals, though I sometimes eat fish and poultry. If I am invited to a country like Colombia, for example, where local fare includes poultry dishes or red meat, for example, their delicious Bandeja Paisa, I would not be able to make myself say no and reject it. I consider myself a 'flexitarian', someone who eats mostly

---

[11] Read more about Dan Buettner and the Blue Zone Communities here: https://www.bluezones.com

a plant-based diet but occasionally eats meat. I was a strict vegetarian for a decade, but no longer adhere to rigid diets. I would rather be free than perfect and enjoy the sweetness of life with moderation. When faced with a health challenge, I usually turn to raw fruits and vegetables. Intermittent fasting is good for some people; there's a lot of literature about it, and our religious ancestors fasted for a reason.

Some people are cautious with what they eat and yet continue to be ill and depressed since their thoughts have toxins worse than any artificial additive, insecticide, or venom. Regardless of what's on your plate, whether you have a banquet or crumbs, give thanks to God. The best seasoning for your meal is gratitude.

Physical environment

Your body is the temple of the soul, and your house is the temple of your body. Look attentively at where you live. What do you see? Bills that are pending, pets uncared for, dirty or broken-down cars, plants that need watering, lack of maintenance, damaged doors, and windows, burned-out light bulbs ... all of these are a clear indicator of disorders or broken pieces in your life. There are financial challenges that change our priorities. Still, chaos in your surrounding environment may mean confusion, lack of discipline, and the inability to make decisions or to let go.

Study the present state of your living surroundings and make the necessary changes to have more order. Find a place for each item, fix whatever is broken, answer pending messages, pay past-due bills, trim the plants, change the batteries, refresh your makeup, recycle all lotion jars. Tidy your house or workspace and see how your mental home automatically clears up.

Simplifying life

We have become a society that is obsessed with buying 'stuff'. Access to any product we fancy is instantaneous. We have substituted common sense with emotional impulses. In this day and age, it is easier and faster to get what we think we need, in some cases even delivered to our door in less than an hour. Instant gratification – the temptation to buy anything we think we need for our status or comfort – is a new type of greed that sellers understand too well. The result is that our houses need to be bigger, and our closets are the size of another room filled with 'stuff' we don't need. In the United States now, renting extra storage rooms has become a necessity to contain all these possessions. We don't only buy – we hoard. The universe recycles; it does not save indefinitely, nor does it waste. Holding on to something you no longer need, goes against the laws of nature. It translates to obstacles in the flow of energy, creating stagnation. Holding on to what is no longer useful sends the wrong message to the universe: *If I am unwilling to let go, I am also unwilling to receive.* Some people save everything, even the clothes they wore in their youth due to indecision (what if) or guilt: 'Once, I didn't have any.' Hoarding, in some instances, could be due to a belief in scarcity. An obsession with saving specific articles, on the other hand, could be hiding an essential message for you. Are those old cookbooks sheltering your dream of becoming a chef?

PRACTICE: BECOMING A MINIMALIST

Saved items that hold your unfulfilled dreams do not propel you into the future, nor do they let you savor the present. Sometimes, we need to update our goals; renew them just as we actualize ourselves, with the focus of evolving from within. Memories trapped in the things we save can make us indecisive by keeping us distracted from new opportunities. Let's breathe fresh air and start anew.

- Choose a month for clearing clutter, including from your desktop. Liberate and dust yourself off – give away and recycle. Let go of that stale smell of the old and replace it with the freshness of flowers. Spring cleaning can be done in any season.
- Take a mental inventory of what works in your life and what doesn't. Do you need two cars? Do you even need a car? A smaller house? I am not saying to let go of dreams and comfort, just of whatever brings you more stress because of its required upkeep. Downgrading could be a blessing in disguise.
- Go over your belongings and make a mental list of what to keep, what to give, what to throw away, and what to recycle. Don't stop until you have touched everything you own with renovating energy. For example, throw away all expired medication, makeup, and food.

If you can let go of whatever serves no purpose in your home, you will see how in the same way, you will let go of people, ideas, and beliefs that have kept you tied down to the past. No wonder the art of decluttering has become a new genre in itself! Letting go of the old is the only way to create newly available space to be filled with a new life.

The environment

Planet Earth is also part of your environment. If you would genuinely like to protect the Earth for future generations, I recommend you make some simple changes to your current lifestyle routines. The ecological 'green' movement is more evidence of the awakening of a new season. You can begin at home with small, ordinary things, such as using less water or electricity, recycling plastic and glass jars, avoiding sprays that are harmful to the ozone layer, walking instead of driving, taking your own reusable bags to the supermarket, or buying eco-friendly cleaning products.

Common sense and verified information will slowly but surely lead you to make better choices as an informed consumer. It would be ideal way to teach your children about these new practices as you educate yourself and learn about products that are good for the environment. I have found alternatives for almost all the products I regularly use.

4

YOUR ABUNDANCE

Nature's currency

THE NORMAL STATE OF BEING IN NATURE IS ABUNDANCE. There is an unlimited number of atoms, minerals, and raw materials available for creation. In its eternal movement, the universe doesn't monopolize, possess, waste, save, or hide its natural resources. It doesn't trade or purchase to later display as a trophy. Instead, it transforms, recycles, and freely gives its resources away for the good of all. Nature is in a constant, harmonious movement under God's wise guidance. Likewise, our natural state is total abundance, and one of its main characteristics is that it flows freely.

> *Look at the birds of the air, for they neither sow nor reap nor gather into barns; yet your heavenly Father feeds them. Are you not of more value than them? Which of you by worrying can add one cubit to his stature?*
>
> — Mathew 6:26

Unfortunately, people often turn their backs on nature, acting in ways opposite to its laws, stealing, monopolizing, and acting selfishly. All of this energy waste is due to our fear of losing something we believe belongs to us: possessions and privileges. We don't realize that with this behavior, we are stopping the natural flow of things and keeping others from enjoying what rightfully belongs to us – creating a great disturbance and imbalance among all available resources. When we are motivated by fear, the energy flow becomes stagnant. It is no coincidence that our monetary exchange token is called *currency*, since it is continually moving, just like a power current, and better yet, our lives are *currently* occurring! A person's state of abundance is not measured by the number of belongings nor by the amount of money in their bank accounts. The biblical quote 'by their fruits you shall know them'[12] refers to a spiritual abundance, not a bank statement.

A genuinely abundant person isn't someone who has the most, but someone who enjoys and appreciates the most. I know wealthy people who are very poor in spirit, and I also know people who are considered poor by our standards, but who are rich and abundant in the way they feel and behave towards others. Material success is transitory. Abundance is permanent. A state of abundance is the result of our attitude towards what abounds, what is overflowing. It is the peace and the certainty of receiving from a never-ending source. It is having the assurance that you will always receive precisely what you need when you need it. Such conviction is the result of trusting God as your true and only source.

---

[12] Matthew 7:16

Following God's Divine design for us will bring the best 'compensation package' by grace, including insurance, universal coverage, and the best health and protection plan, which includes an abundance of coverage for yourself and your loved ones. Whoever has more in one area should help the ones who lack in another; this applies to emotional, mental, and spiritual wealth.

What determines your thoughts on money?

Do you know what your underlying beliefs are regarding the prosperity you can achieve or deserve? Your beliefs undoubtedly come from lessons learned in the past. We learn wonderful lessons from our family that build our values, but many times we also learn beliefs that can be harmful. Over the years, your social and physical environment have contributed to creating mental myths, limits, and subconscious lessons that rule your behavior, silently influencing your daily decisions.

A child who saw his parents suffering from a loss or lack of basic needs could develop an inner fear that will create behaviors that are inconsistent with abundant life, like the habit of saving unusable items beyond measure, or the need to save on items impulsively when shopping for groceries. The reality is that advantages in wealth and education early in life make a difference. Nevertheless, even in the case of having been born with disadvantages, there's always an opportunity to succeed if we have the right attitude and connect with our purpose. It is essential to clarify that success doesn't mean the same to everyone, and that material prosperity is not the only measure of accomplishment. Material success without a life of meaning is a failure. We need an abundant soul, and in this sense, it begins in the heart.

> *... what comes out of the mouth proceeds from the heart, and this defiles a person.*
>
> — Mathew 15:11

First Class Disappointment

Once, while I was boarding a plane, I noticed a very charming, innocent boy sitting down comfortably in a first-class seat. He couldn't have been more than seven. Suddenly, his mother pulled him by the arm, abruptly yelling, 'Whoever told you that you could have a seat in first class, kid? No way! Stop dreaming!' The boy's smile vanished immediately – so did his dream. He had been awakened abruptly from his daydreaming and sadly walked away, looking back at the seat he left behind as if saying, 'Lucky people who get to sit in such big and comfortable seats.'

This seemingly innocent event may have created a false belief in the young child, telling him he would never be significant enough to sit where first-class passengers sit. Consequently, he might go through life, wrongly thinking that the possibility is not for him. The opposite could also be true though; our little hero could choose to do whatever it takes in his life to be able to one day sit in a first-class seat, showing his mother she was wrong.

The society also puts limits on people of color, certain social class, and immigrants. We have to break away from these patterns of prejudice and stereotypes, and this begins by breaking free of the limitations we have accepted as facts. How often have we been the teacher, the parent, or the friend who, with all the best intentions in mind, acted in the same manner and put an end to someone else's dreams with a negative remark? Our own set of beliefs can perpetuate a negative relationship with abundance.

Myths and Money

First myth: False humility

The mistaken belief that financial success determines your degree of humility is one of the biggest enemies of prosperity. How often do we hear this statement of false modesty: 'I'm not interested in money,' or 'I don't care about money'?

Money should not be your idol or first motivation in life, but it cannot be overlooked. Money is our *energy exchange program,* a fundamental aspect of our way of doing business here on Earth.

True humility is born out of the awareness that we are all one and equal before God. We are similar to the fruit from the branch; some branches are higher than others. However, we acknowledge our mutual dependence on God; since, on our own we can do nothing. To be humble is to remember that nothing is permanent: sooner or later, we must depart from this planet, leaving all of our dear earthly possessions behind.

The fact that everything changes and eventually comes to an end should be humbling enough. We are simple caretakers with temporary custody of imaginary properties and belongings – possessions that will be in our hands for only a short time. Regardless of who you are or what you have, hundred years from now, someone else will be enjoying what you think will never end – if it still exists.

True humility is the antidote to the ego. It is to listen without searching for every opportunity to talk about ourselves and our significant assets. To be meek is to be interested in others and to help them unconditionally. When we are truly humble, we avoid taking pride in what we do or have. Our real Self shines from within; it doesn't need to have a sense of entitlement, demanding to be the first in line or asking for special treatment. Real power doesn't call attention to itself; it waits, observing patiently, since the truly powerful are known for their temperance. They know that everything comes to pass. If we act with love and without attachment, the fruits of our actions will arrive effortlessly.

Blessed are the meek.

— Mathew 5:5

False pride, however, interrupts the flow of energy in the opposite direction as well. When we don't allow ourselves to accept a gift from others, it prevents us from receiving the help we might need. Thinking that we are *not enough* can deceive us by wearing the mask of false humbleness by saying – 'No, thank you, I don't need help.' When someone offers you a gift, information, maybe a smile or a glass of water – accept it. Many times, we reject help because of embarrassment or pride. When we act this way, we rob the other person of an opportunity to give. It also deprives us of the chance to receive as well. When someone comes to give you a present, remember, it is God giving you His gift.

Second myth: If I win, someone has to lose

Feeling guilty for being prosperous and the fear of success are two roadblocks that stop the flow of abundance. When we refuse to live to the highest possible expression of our inner Self, we are denying others the opportunity to receive your gifts and inspirations. This belief can then result in the experience of guilt. Once prosperity is achieved with integrity, and supported by the balance of giving back accordingly, personal success does not steal the opportunity from others to earn their bread. Quite the opposite – your example may inspire and help others to do their best.

Third myth: There isn't enough

This belief can result in fear of losing money. We forget this world was created in perfect balance, and its resources are sufficient for all. It is precisely the fear of losing control over those resources that have brought greed and imbalance to rule. Fear will create an attachment to money and cause you to lose it. If under these circumstances, you are still fortunate enough to keep it, fear can rob you of your peace and the ability to enjoy healthy relationships and what you have earned. Attachment to money is the result of the fear of losing security, and it is responsible for all sorts of abuses and bad choices. Wealth and abundance both come from God. Surrender all your gifts to Him, and regardless of the amount, you will always feel that you have enough.

Fourth myth: Money is the root of all evil

Money is not the root of evil, but our attachment and fear of losing it are. Many automatically portray rich people as corrupt persons, but money won't necessarily turn honest people into dishonest ones. Luckily, these are stereotypes and not the norm. However, sudden wealth can trigger and increase preexisting negative qualities.

I once asked Dada if abundance was as bad as people said. Can a rich person get into Heaven? He smiled and said, 'Do not worry, my child. Money and abundance won't hurt you on the spiritual journey as long as you are the master of the money and not the other way around.' Master your money wisely and never let it have power over you. The outcome of the horrible inequalities in the realities and the politics of the world is that the poor are kept poor and the rich get richer, but if anyone can awaken to the possibility of a better life, let's help them with education and meals while they get on their feet. Governments and businesses are unfair when they perpetuate negative conditions by diminishing the needs of the poor. In an interview, Mother Teresa reminded us that poor people are good people and that many of them are happy and content even in adverse conditions. The worst poverty is the poorness of spirit, she had said. You can give a poor person a blanket, and it will stop the cold, but a rich person who is poor of spirit is not that simple to comfort.[13]

---

13 'Firing Line with William F. Buckley, Jr.: Mother Teresa Talks with William F. Buckley, Jr.' YouTube video. 3 February 2017. https://www.youtube.com/watch?v=3__jvGa5L6Y.

THE STORY OF THE CAMEL AND THE EYE OF THE NEEDLE

Jesus said: 'It is easier for a camel to go through the eye of a needle than for a rich man to enter the kingdom of Heaven.'[14] The question is, what is the real meaning? There are different interpretations of this lesson. One of them sees the eye of the needle as the entrance gate of a city; camels needed their loads removed before they could pass through a small gate. According to another, the word for 'camel' in Aramaic, the original tongue of the biblical writings, also means 'rope'. Both interpretations make it clear that no one who puts his riches before God will find happiness or enter the kingdom of Heaven. But how do you surrender your wealth to God?

PAXSON, A REAL-LIFE STORY

Bud Paxson, founder of the cable TV purchasing chain Home Shopping Network, one of the largest in the US, tells his experience in his memoir, *Threading the Needle: The PAX NET Story*. The business was everything to Bud, but he soon discovered that the price for increasing his riches without meaning was way too high. According to his memoir, on a beautiful, apparently harmonious Christmas evening, his wife surprised him with the sad words, 'I'm leaving you.'[15]

---

[14] Matthew 19:24

[15] Lowell 'Bud' Paxson, *Threading the Needle: The PAX NET Story* (New York: HarperCollins, 1998), p. 87.

Bud plunged into the 'dark night of the soul' after his wife's decision to leave him. Later, one evening while staying alone in the most luxurious suite of a famous hotel in Las Vegas, he realized in tears that no money was worth anything without the love and presence of the people he loved. Though a multimillionaire, Bud had fallen into spiritual bankruptcy. That very night, he searched desperately for a Bible in the hotel room and fell asleep reading the Scripture. The next day he felt different, as if a miracle had occurred. Without knowing it, Bud had surrendered his will to God that night, and miracles began to happen.

After the experience, Bud sold his stock in the TV shopping chain and rebuilt his life and eventually remarried. He also decided to devote all of his talents to God. Bud founded the PAX TV family network and, among other businesses, created the Christian Network, a notable non-profit chain that reached over sixty-three million Americans for more than eighteen years. Bud Paxson concluded that as long as you surrender all of your talents to God and His cause, He will always compensate you. Regardless of what religion you profess, if you resolve to pursue your calling with love and joy, and walk according to God's plan for your life, without any doubt, you will receive the adequate reward: abundance in all areas. The most important is the abundance of spirit.

Why is money lost?

There are two ways of losing money. One is to lose it after having it, as in bankruptcy. The other way is to feel a permanent dissatisfaction even when we have all we have ever wanted. There are several possible reasons behind losing entire fortunes. There are financial cycles and outside circumstances that can happen – as in an economic crash. Nevertheless, other times we lose money because of fear, greed, or waste. Not infrequently, we may experience losses due to bad decisions resulting from lack of self-esteem, need for approval, wrong religious beliefs (guilt), need for power or lack of integrity. A common reason for loss happens when there's an imbalance between giving and receiving – either by giving too much or by giving too little. Failure to be grateful and not giving credit to the Divine source is repellent to abundance. God doesn't take our money away, but not being grateful is the same as not being present. Distraction is another way to lose a gift or property. Another cause of losing money, fortune, and income is not living a life of purpose and not occupying your rightful place in the Divine plan. Remember that nature makes the best use of all its resources and does not waste any. How many times have we lost a position we found 'comfortable'? How many times has losing a long-term job become a blessing when we had to reinvent ourselves? If your gifts are not being used to the best of your capabilities, or are not part of humanity's common good, you might be forced in the right direction.

The seeds for abundance

Abundance is your ability to enjoy what you have regardless of how much you own. In contrast, prosperity is an increase in the fruits of your labor, be they spiritual, emotional, or physical ones. Poverty and wealth refer to more than just the material world. You may experience a lack of wealth in your spiritual life, health, family, love, or ability to serve others regardless of what you own physically. Never forget that God wants you to prosper in all areas.

> *Beloved, I pray that you be prosperous in everything, just as your soul prospers, and that you may have good health.*
>
> — 3 John 1:2

To paraphrase C.S. Lewis: *we can't choose where we begin in life, but we can always choose where we will end.* Your progress is the exact result of the seeds previously planted in different areas of your life. There is no mistake in the universe. Seeds begin in the form of a thought, become a belief, and later result in your actions, which should always be consistent with that of an abundant person. Negative thoughts don't create problems as much as negative beliefs planted in our subconscious. Following is a list of beautiful seeds you can plant that will provide abundance and prosperity in the different areas of your life.

- **First seed:** Observe yourself. Identify the myths and beliefs you hold about worth and merit, and change your conscience. In your journal, draw two columns. Write your old views in the first, and next to it, write the new belief. Modify beliefs like: 'I'm not enough, I don't deserve, and I'm not worthy,' which each pertain to scarcity, whether you have little or much. Plant a new thought today: 'I deserve it. I am the son/daughter of God. I'm enough, I matter, and I'm worth it. God fulfills all my needs.' These affirmations will change your experience regarding your abundance. You may notice some resistance but continue with this new affirmation.

- **Second seed:** Take responsibility for your past errors. Pay your accounts on all fronts. Forgive yourself, both for bad decisions as well as any excesses. Forgive the people who deceived you or have taken anything from you. When you forgive, you let go of the vengeful thoughts that occupy the space of creative ones.
- **Third seed:** Be grateful. Write a list of the presents God has given you already. Look closely: they are everywhere. The sun, oxygen, your children, health, your talents, and other gifts ... Give thanks for the gifts you have today to receive the gifts of the morrow.
- **Fourth seed:** Surrender your finances and possessions to God. It is an area we commonly resist surrendering, though it is He who gives us all our abundance. Repeat the following: 'God, may Your Will be done with my finances. May my goods be put to use for Your highest expression.' After this petition, you should live worry-free concerning your money.
- **Fifth seed:** Use your talents to help humanity. My teacher Alexander Everett once said: 'If you want a million, you must first give a million in service.'
- **Sixth seed:** Give to yourself by saving, but don't forget to give a tenth of your profits to a cause you consider important.
- **Seventh seed:** Act now. Start wherever you are. Organize yourself, pay your bills, save, invest, clear your debts, and collect from debtors. Take a course; education is an advantage. Begin to manage what you have,

responsively, regardless of the amount. Whoever cannot handle one hundred dollars correctly cannot handle one hundred thousand, let alone one million. Visualize a plan and act consistently with your new attitude of abundance.

- **Eighth seed:** Practice generosity. More than sharing material things, kindness is about giving the best of yourself each time. Money is not the only tool you can use to invest in others. You can also provide resources and information. You can lend a hand, smile at others freely, and offer your friendship. See how eager you are to give a compliment, say thanks, be kind, show appreciation for a job well done. Give a standing ovation, work extra hours with no expectations, leave a note with a beautiful thought, be one with your word. Share a pie with a neighbor and give generous tips! They will all come back to you in blessings.

  Be generous to your Self. Value who you are. Give yourself time, rest, vacation, give yourself a treat. Value your Self, and value the inner Self in others, not their possessions. We should love people for who they are, not for what they can give us.

If you feel your business is a burden, simplify things a little. Value the simple things in life. One simple picnic at a park may be more satisfying than the most luxurious hotel's feast. Value the things you have, and don't get distracted by what you feel is missing.

Value the people near to you: your friends, your companion, a dear one, your partner, and life itself. We never know how long they are going to be with us. Giving a tight hug, saying thank you, smiling, bringing a flower, and sharing a sunset, all are priceless. Enjoy these gifts. Give of yourself without expectations, and the universe will compensate you accordingly.

5

YOUR SPIRITUALITY

WHEN WE TALK ABOUT SPIRITUALITY, A PICTURE OF AN invisible reality comes to mind. Nevertheless, everything in our universe, even the material, is spiritual at the core. With this perspective, money and holy water are both spiritual – just as a businessman and a priest are. Both the seen and the unseen are holy. The objective or material world is dependent on and affected by the subjective or spiritual world. We wage a silent war, between those who call themselves religious and those who define their path as spiritual. However, we cannot stop being spiritual. Spirituality is not a religion; it is a personal quest for transcendence. Religion is the set of beliefs we choose; in most cases, your environment determines your faith. Religions are not meant to be exclusive clubs or separate human beings. Consciously 'living' the right lessons of religion is more important than 'practicing rituals'. However, rituals can assist us in becoming closer to our immediate family, our community, and God.

I am not against religion. On the contrary, religion is a language, and everyone has a right to relate to God with their own words and symbols. Every religion has a light side, and also a dark side. The light is lost when the darkness of fanaticism casts its shadow over any set of reasonable beliefs.

There are many paths to reach God. Each person chooses the practice he needs in each stage of his life's evolution. We all go through different stages of faith. We cannot judge or criticize others' practices, clothes, rites, or languages simply because they appear different from our own. When I talk about spirituality, it is beyond creeds and dogmas. It is the peaceful way each of us chooses to express his or her relationship with God.

WHERE IS GOD?

The Talmud includes a conversation between the Roman emperor Hadrian and Rabbi Joshua.[16]

The emperor asked, 'You say you talk to God every day, but where is your God? I want to see Him.'

'That is impossible,' said the rabbi.

Quite upset, the emperor replied, 'How can you expect me to believe in a God I cannot see?'

The rabbi then told the emperor, 'Focus your eyes directly on the sun.'

'I … cannot,' replied the emperor.

The rabbi smiled and said, 'How can you expect to see

---

[16] As told by Dada J.P. Vaswani in *The Way of Abhyasa: How to Meditate.*

God if you cannot even look at the sun, which is only a mere servant of His?'

God

There is only one God. However, each person visualizes Him in a way that he can understand. An aborigine may picture God as the sun. A western artist may depict Him as a white man surrounded by angels, while a scientist may describe Him as a great energy matrix in movement.

My way of seeing God is simple: God is One. He is Mother and Father; God is all. I used to believe in a distant God. I thought He was severe and unforgiving. He resembled an emotional dictator more than a loving father. My old god behaved and reacted just as a human would, demanding devotion and punishing whoever did not obey and adore Him. In my mind, God had a white beard and ruled over me from the heavens. I believed He was forever judging me from high above.

Today my vision is different. I see a loving, omnipresent, omniscient God – inclusive, simultaneously existing everywhere, ageless and timeless. Now I see God as the Creator and also as the womb of the universe and its laws, though in His unmanifested form, He is not touched by our physical world. God's nature might be beyond my capacity to understand, yet that does not keep me from experiencing Him in a very personal way, inside my heart.

Are we god?

We are sons and daughters of God, but we have forgotten. This psalm is a beautiful reminder:

> *They do not know or understand; they wander in the darkness; all the foundations of the earth are shaken. I have said, 'You are gods'; you are all sons of the Most High.*
>
> — Psalms 82:6

Jesus even quoted this psalm in his defense, as a reminder to the naysayers: 'Isn't it written in your Laws, "You are gods?"' We must remember that a drop of water from the sea cannot be defined as the ocean itself, but only as a part of it. The drop of water cannot be described as a separate entity, either. Therefore, each drop in the ocean is a holographic replica of the whole, each made in the image and likeness of the sea. Even though the drop is not the totality of the ocean, it is an authentic mirror, made from the same substance. Likewise, while it is true that we are the Divine *image and likeness of God*, we are not God, but a part of Him, His beloved children. A priest once told me: 'It is impossible to lose our image of God, but it is easy to lose His likeness.'

> *God manifests and expresses Himself through my being. He IS and sees through my very eyes. He is the reason for my existence as much as I am His reason to be. He is my guiding light, my north, and my plan. He knows the way. He is the Way.*

The essence of spirituality

Some people need to see the evidence of religiosity in another; however, we do not need to have a title, dress, or speak in a certain way to appear as spiritual. The essence of spirituality rests in our honest quest for what lies beyond us. Therefore, we need to be consistent in our message. Practicing rituals is not enough to convey honesty. Honesty in spirituality walks side by side with our intentions, together with our loving actions. Good deeds don't need to be on public display. A simple, honest embrace of another human being or a piece of bread given to a homeless person in private can be the highest form of praise to God, and therefore, of spirituality. People who are spiritually conscious don't need to impress anyone with their knowledge either. They know information is not exclusive, and God is indescribable in words. Thus, they choose to be humble at all times.

Awakening others

Inspiring others to connect to their inner light is the most powerful message you can share. *Being* is more important than convincing. It is important to remember that inspiring others does not mean that everyone must listen or do what you do. Many do not find our message compatible with their beliefs or are already practicing a form of faith that suits them better in their own communities. Frequently, others can also become your teacher if you are willing to listen.

Don't force your message. Just plant the seed. Your example speaks louder than words. It is also important to realize that we can have a positive effect through the energy we put forth, given that everything in the universe is connected. According to my teacher Dada, there are people who, when gathered in a group, can help others connect to God's energy. He used to call them *poles* because they act as magnets, helping others to connect with God's force.

BE LIKE A PIANO TUNER

In 1665, Dutch scientist Christiaan Huygens discovered that if he placed two pendulum clocks side by side, but at different rhythms, they would soon synchronize to the same time and pace. He called this phenomenon 'sympathetic vibrations'. Something similar occurs with the tuning fork used to fine-tune the piano. When we place one next to another while it is still vibrating, the second one will start vibrating at the same rate.

Fish swim in the same rhythm, birds synchronize their flight, and in the same manner, humans affect one another – not just each other's hate and aggression frequencies, but also the waves of peace and universal love. One selfish leader can contaminate the whole world with hate. The world of vibrations is no longer an exclusive reality of the sixties.[17] When you are connected, and in harmony with God, His higher frequency always protects you. To become an emissary of spiritual change, we don't need to be perfect. Still, we must strive to keep a conscious connection with God. We run all sorts of personal, material, and spiritual risks for ourselves and others when we fail to connect to God before helping others.

Agents of spiritual change

The gift to inspire others through unconditional random acts of kindness is the true meaning of loving one

---

[17] For a modern take on vibrations, see 'The Hippies Were Right: It's All about Vibrations, Man!' on Scientific American Blog Network by Tam Hunt, posted on 5 December 2018. https://blogs.scientificamerican.com/observations/the-hippies-were-right-its-all-about-vibrations-man/.

another. Those who are genuine agents of spiritual change demonstrate this gift through their integrity and honesty in the way they treat others, including those with whom they disagree. Spiritual people are not necessarily perfect people; no one in this world is. They will surely make mistakes, but even in the face of their errors, they will be honest and strive to correct them. Spiritual teachers live in a constant learning process with challenges and falls, which usually relate to the same lessons they come to teach.

A truly spiritual person will show reverence for others and the simple things in life. He works to serve others without using his own knowledge for personal gain or privileges. He simply acts in a way that is consistent with what he says, does, and thinks.

False prophets

None of us living in this world is entirely free of shadows and errors. Therefore, it is wise to be aware of false prophets. We live in a time of high emotional vulnerability, and many are more susceptible to falling prey to all sorts of psychological traps, cults, and disguises.

Beware of false leaders! Always demand transparency and respect. Be suspicious if they ask for money or possessions. In the same manner, be vigilant whenever any leader tries to separate you from your family, makes a sexual advance, or requests a problematic, dangerous, or senseless feat to prove your faith. Lastly, be careful of giving blind devotion to any earthly leader. I urge you to be cautious, not necessarily to distrust everyone but to be discerning. You always have the right to ask questions. Trust and listen to your intuition.

Questions about the afterlife

The philosophies of many religions explain life after death in different ways. I respect different views and enjoy interfaith dialogue. Some state that after death, the soul continues to evolve by being reborn in another body. However, other religions believe that the soul evolves towards other worlds or planes. Most believe in either Heaven or Hell, or both. Still others deny reincarnation and explain past life memories as the result of a unified collective memory.

There is a common denominator that brings most of these theories together – in the afterlife, we all return to God, our source. Explaining the concept of life after death or reincarnation can be a real challenge in the multidimensional complexity of our universe. We live in a linear world, but eternity is a state that is outside of time. In St. Augustine's words, forever is not a long time but a place without time. How can you explain this miracle in terms that make sense? In matters of the spirit, I would rather stay open with a question than closed with an answer. I know for sure that even though I cannot know the details, I trust that there is a perfect plan based on love at work. I believe the soul survives the body, keeps its identity and reunites with loved ones until we return to God, who is beyond our laws of space and time. I believe God is immensely loving, all-knowing, compassionate, and forgiving. That even for the worst of us, if we choose it, He has a plan for forgiveness and redemption. The rest is a mystery.

We can only surrender, be grateful, forgive ourselves and others and connect to His plan and His inner peace, allowing Him to show us the way. It is not necessary to understand all the details in this Divine plan. During a conference I attended, someone asked the Dalai Lama if he remembered his past lives. He jokingly replied, 'The truth is that I can't even remember what I had for breakfast today.' Tibetan Buddhists are firm believers in reincarnation. With his comment, however, the Dalai Lama showed us the futility of trying to find answers in the past, be it in childhood or earlier in other lives. The answers to our questions are most likely in the present.

Values are universal

Universal values, or *higher virtues*, are not exclusive to Eastern or Western religions; they are common to believers and non-believers. Some examples are:

- **Gratitude:** Being grateful is accepting that everything, absolutely everything, is a gift from God. The sun, the moon, the rain, everything is God's grace. We find something of value in every experience, regardless of its nature.
- **Integrity:** Being a person of integrity is always to follow our inner truth, our Divine compass. It is to be clear about our real intentions at all times. If we consciously intend to walk in God's Will, we will live in integrity.
- **Empathy:** Having empathy is accepting that we are far from perfect, that we make mistakes, and that at some point, we may suffer and feel pain just as others do. Empathy frees us from prejudices and being judgmental, bringing us closer to others.

- **Compassion***:* Our capacity to share and feel love for all humanity matures when we become an instrument of God. Compassion is born in moments of need when the Divine Love of God can flow from our hearts towards others to assist in healing. It recognizes that everyone is your brother and that ultimately, we are all part of the same God.
- **Will***:* God gave us an unconditional power to choose right from wrong. Our own will is stronger when we surrender our desires – when His Will rests above everything else in our priorities.
- **Service***:* The highest form of purpose in our lives is to be of service. An act of service happens every time we respond without expecting something in return. It should not be confused with duty, or obligation, or a way to receive payment or recognition. Service is the natural way to share and respond to the needs of others. Trees give us their fruits and birds give us their songs without any reason other than the pleasure of giving. Selfless service to others is the highest form of praise to God.
- **Leadership***:* A leader is one who uses his skills to bring about the best in others. He uses his gifts to inspire and show the way to God. To be a good leader, one must first learn to be a good disciple.
- **Enthusiasm***:* The very word comes from the Greek root *en-Theos*, meaning 'in God'. When you are connected, your energy comes straight from the source, and you are full of His essence. Your real purpose expresses itself with energy when you are feeling 'en-thusiastic'; that is when you are 'in God'.

- **Amazement***:* Being amazed is to be able to see everything with the innocent eyes of a child. Those who marvel at the simple things have found the door to Heaven. Jesus taught this lesson. Amazement is looking at everything anew, with joy and a smile. It is when you can experience reverence towards everything around you, recognizing the entirety as part of God. It is tasting life with all the senses, without thought, memory, or judgment, as if experiencing everything for the first time.
- **Non-attachment***:* Non-attachment is letting go of your ego's wants and desires for what God has in His Holy Mind for us. It is to be aware of the temporary and fleeting nature of life, understanding, and accepting that everything changes, transforms, and ends as part of the Divine order.
- **Patience***:* Patience is the science of being calm in the middle of turmoil. To have patience, we must first have faith, which means knowing that everything has precise timing and order. Fruits have their process to ripen. If you eat the fruit before it is time, it will leave a sour taste in your mouth.
- **Sweetness***:* Practicing the art of gentleness is to clothe every word, thought, and deed with the honey of love.

THE BUDDHA AND THE MANGO

A group of followers pleaded with the Buddha for a spiritual message. The Buddha remained silent and picked a ripe mango fruit and held it in his hands. The followers clamored for a spiritual message for a second time. Again, the Buddha remained silent with the mango still in his hands. For a third time, the followers demanded a lesson, yet they received a quiet Buddha and the vision of the mango. After a long pause, the Buddha replied, 'Three times I have shown you the secret to spirituality, but you still do not see it. Today's lesson is that you become as sweet as this mango fruit in your gestures, words, and deeds.'[18]

Are you meditating or ruminating?

When someone asks me how much time I meditate, I reply: I try to meditate all the time, at least while awake. I am referring to being conscious, present, and aware of the presence of God throughout the day. Prayer and meditation require a continuous communion with God. In the letters of Paul, he instructed us: 'Rejoice at all times. Pray without ceasing. Give thanks in every circumstance.'[19]

Learning to meditate can be very frustrating for a fidgety person like me. What many people mistakenly call meditation is only sitting to ruminate and dwell on each problem, making everything worse by watching it on the big screen of their minds! I don't find that practice very positive. There is a variety of meditation and relaxation techniques. I invite you to experiment with different practices until you find the one that is best for you.

PRACTICE: SIMPLE MEDITATION

The most common meditation is to simply sit comfortably with your spine straight and supported, if needed, by a

[18] I heard this story at the feet of my dear teacher Dada J.P. Vaswani

[19] Thessalonians 5:16

timer set for five, ten, or fifteen minutes. Close your eyes and pay attention to your breathing. Notice thoughts but don't follow them; just return your attention to your breath after each interruption of ideas, memories, plans, or warnings. Even though this sounds simple, it is not always that easy. Be persistent.

PRACTICE: BREATH OF LIGHT

An old meditation technique from the East inspires the idea of breathing in from the diaphragm. Paying attention to your breathing is very powerful since you cannot focus on your thoughts and your breathing at the same time. The spaces within our thoughts are momentary windows to the soul, for God talks to you through the curtains of your silence. There is no right or wrong time to practice meditation, but it is particularly useful to do it daily when feeling agitated or during other stressful times.

1. Find a quiet spot, and make sure you will not be disturbed. Sit up straight; use pillows, if needed, to help you find a comfortable but erect spine position. Locate your diaphragm, the muscle under your ribs. Bring your diaphragm up and down with the air you breathe in and out. See your stomach rise and fall.
2. Mentally breathe in light. Keep the breath in for two seconds, or as long as needed, to get into a harmonious rhythm.
3. Exhale through your nose. Inhalations, though full, should be a little shorter than exhalations.

4. Visualize the air flowing up and down through a bright tunnel of light, purifying all of your body, from the sacral part of your spine to the crown of your head. Smile after breathing out.
5. You may guide your breath by repeating the name of your source of Divine inspiration. For example, if using the name of Jesus, you can say the first syllable 'Je' while breathing in and 'sus' while exhaling. You can use the name or word that inspires you in your own tradition. Try to do anywhere between 10 to 108 repetitions, depending on your needs, ability, and schedule. You can repeat this sequence as many times as you find necessary at any given time. You can also use a tool to help you concentrate, such as a rosary or a mala, a string of beads used by Hindus and Buddhists, or a *tasbih*, the Muslim prayer beads. The Eastern Christians used a prayer rope called a *komboskini* in Greek. The main religions agree that keeping track of your repetitions improves your concentration.

6

YOUR SERVICE

WE OFTEN HEAR THAT SERVICE TO OTHERS IS THE WAY to happiness. However, giving to others should be done without expecting a reward, be it gratitude, recognition, admiration, money, benefits, or privileges. When we ask ourselves the right questions, true service becomes natural: 'How can I be useful?' and 'How may I serve?' sets the right state of mind to relate to others. The most authentic act of service is when you allow God to work through you, as St. Francis of Assisi said, 'to make you an instrument of His plan.' For our lives to have meaning, we need to have a purpose. 'Being, living, and serving' is not only a technique for happiness; it is a way of life. 'A life not lived for others is not a life,' a quote attributed to Mother Teresa of Calcutta, says it well. When you find your true gift and honor your natural abilities, expressing your gift will be inevitable.

Once I asked a friend, Jaime Jaramillo 'Papa Jaime', a recipient of the World Peace Award for rescuing thousands of children from the sewers in Bogotá, 'How can you go into such dirt and stench?' Jaime replied, 'How could I not? How can I not help a defenseless child?'

A real surgeon isn't bothered by blood; children don't upset a devoted elementary school teacher; numbers don't overwhelm a true accountant. In nature, we see how camels are not affected by the heat of the desert, nor are eagles afraid of heights. They simply express their natural 'self' in whatever place they need to be, expecting nothing in return. Every sentient being was born with their element. Not every bird is meant to be an eagle, and not every person is meant to be a surgeon.

We all have a role in this life. Some come to give with their hands, some come to heal, others come to teach, and others to create. Some people are here to organize, others to build, some to communicate, and others to build bridges between beings. Some of us serve in health, while others serve in sickness; therefore, no gift is better or worse than another. It is essential to discover your gift and find a way to share it naturally with others. As Papa Jaime says, *if you serve from love, instead of pity or suffering, you will never feel uncomfortable helping anyone.*

Jaime echoed the words of Pope John Paul II, 'No one is too poor to give or too rich to receive.'

When you are serving others, you serve God. Give with all your heart yet remain unattached to results. Like an instrument, surrender to God any need to be recognized for any merit of your own. In return, give all the credit to God.

Faithful people of service act without expectations to change the world. They don't fight against war; they only walk towards peace. Rosa Parks did not throw stones at racists. She simply sat on the seat that she deserved, a place previously assigned only to white-skinned people. A reporter who is said to have once asked Mother Teresa of Calcutta why she did not participate in anti-war demonstrations received the following reply: 'I will never do that, but as soon as you have a pro-peace rally, I'll be there.'

To be able to help others, your own house must be in order. Learn to take good care of yourself first, make sure you rest, and learn to heal. Once healthy, find your gift and give away the service you naturally came to provide.

Oprah Winfrey, a renowned television personality who has devoted her life to inspiring others, shared this powerful prayer: 'Use me, God. Show me how to take who I am, who I want to be, and what I can do, and use it for a purpose greater than myself.'[20] How beautiful it is to ask God to make us an instrument in ways that are unimaginable to us. Oprah knows very well that words in the form of this prayer are powerful. Her life is a clear example of personal achievement and selfless service. A black woman of humble beginnings who has the right vision has become an instrument as a TV icon; she has inspired millions of people to better themselves through her programs.

[20] 'What Oprah Knows for Sure About Finding Success,' Oprah.com, https://www.oprah.com/omagazine/what-oprah-knows-for-sure-about-finding-success.

7

YOUR LOVE RELATIONSHIPS

TRUE LOVE IS A SOOTHING BALM. THE POWER THAT MOVES the universe and the substance that fuels all our dreams. Love is absolute beauty. Love is the light, the word, the silence, and the logos. Love is God's embrace expressed as the caress of the wind. Love is the fragrance of God. Love gives strength to the rock and the emptiness to the void. It is in the alpha and the omega; the director of the spirit that gives life to life itself. Love is God.

> *True love is what you experience when you realize that everything, absolutely everything, originates from the Divine.*

True love has no seasons because it is unchanging, eternal, ageless. Love is immutable and beyond the laws of time and space. You cannot obtain it from others because it already lives within you. You cannot give it to others because it already lives within them. Still, we can remind each other of God's love to us. For this reason, love does not depend on anything or anyone. You can simply experience it from within yourself, and the only way to share it is through your authentic Self. Only by being connected to God and genuinely being 'yourself' can you experience and emanate true love.

Finding 'the one'

Many people believe in the existence of soul mates. All our lives, we search for that perfect love, that special someone who will love, admire, and accept us just as we are. We expect this person to have the same mission and life interests, see inside and understand without words, without judgments. Our soul mate will always tell us the truth, but without criticism. He will support our craziest dreams, love us on our worst days, and be our loyal companion during those endless months of old age. We search for someone who can love us even after our beauty, talents, and vitality have all diminished.

Such grand love is possible, but before searching for the ideal outside of yourself, you must first learn to experience it from within. You do this by finding the same love inside yourself that you are searching for on the outside. You must love yourself on your worst days: forgive your errors and mistakes; overlook your forgetfulness; minimize your limitations; and celebrate your talents and gifts. You must give yourself support in your old age and love yourself even after your beauty, talents, and vitality have diminished.

The road to that special love is the same as the quest to find your Self. If you persist in practicing meditation, contemplation, and the connection with God, you will find yourself vibrating with love, gratitude, and acceptance. It will be inevitable that you experience true love in your life.

Remember that true love can be felt, even if you don't have a life partner. It is the law: others will treat you in the same manner as you treat your Self and others.

A season to love

One falls in love in a magical instant when one awakens in another person a pure feeling of unconditional love, filled with new hopes and fresh possibilities. The chemistry that provokes love at first sight creates a hormonal revolution of involuntary and inexplicable feelings. Still, love is beyond chemistry. The spark of love can happen anywhere – and at the most inconvenient times. Love is a mystery.

Many spend their lives dreaming of meeting the 'one', a long-awaited reunion with an awakened soul. Perhaps this soul will be the one we made a pact with while in Heaven, a promise of love to meet later amid all the confusion of this world. Finding this love is our final reward after so much searching, heartbreaks, incompatibility, and loneliness. We are confident that this person, our twin flame, is the answer that will put an end to every past experience of manipulation, demands, duties, and doubts we have had. With our soul mate, we can finally let go of our fears and find the freedom to be our own Self.

Dada Vaswani always reminded me that nothing is completely determined, yet he assured me that both the day we die and the day we find our partner on Earth are predestined. Therefore, according to destiny, your soul mate will come to you without effort.

In other words, your ideal mate will simply arrive when you resonate with him, when both your characters and gifts complement one another. With the same logic, we may also choose to leave a relationship when one of both has learned the lesson, when the purpose is complete, when the flame dims, when the admiration and respect are lost, or of course, 'until death does us apart'.

We fall in love when we see ourselves reflected in the positive character traits of another. When love manifests as pure inspiration and admiration, we can say that we are falling in love with ourselves. We are attracted to the virtues we believe we lack, those we wish we possessed, or those we already own yet haven't been able to recognize within ourselves.

Sometimes love is inconvenient. It may arrive at the wrong time or with a seemingly wrong partner. Love is beyond seasons, beyond explanations. Never judge someone who has fallen in love, regardless of the situation. What are love songs if not for all the impossible and unrequited loves that were not meant to last?

> *Love is love is love is love is love is love is love is love*
> *cannot be killed or swept aside ...*[21]
>
> — Lin-Manuel Miranda

The true purpose of relationships is to be a mirror of one another. Our partner may show us what may be lacking in our own lives and teach us how to fulfill or complete what is missing, and vice versa. All of our experiences in

---

[21] Sonnet from the 2016 Tony Awards; written for his wife, Vanessa Nadal, as well as the victims of the 2016 Orlando shooting massacre, which left fifty people dead.

relationships are of value. We can learn even from the painful ones such as those involving jealousy and betrayal, for they show us a mirror of our areas for growth. As we awaken into consciousness, we will realize that in order to learn, we do not need to suffer anymore.

Can you love yourself?

'Self-love' is not just a phrase. When I ask someone, 'Do you love yourself?' I always hear an 'Of course I do!' But our lives do not lie, and they too often show us a faithful reflection of the real answer. If you feel your partner does not value you, look deep to find the ways you do not value yourself. If you think your partner is not committed to you, see how you do not commit to your own life. The behavior of another is not our fault, but our choice to stay or walk away is always in our hands. We unknowingly teach others how to treat us by what we habitually tolerate.

'Love thy brother as thyself,' but pay attention: not more than you love yourself. For when Jesus says, 'Love thy brother as thyself,' means that to love another, you must first be able to love yourself. You can love another as you love yourself, yes, but not more than you love yourself.

Self-love is not the same as narcissism, which happens when self-love goes from the Self to the extreme of selfishness. When we use love to get something in return, it is not a gift but a transaction. Some egotistical personalities have a bigger love for things than for people. Our personal relationships and the way we live are a reflection of the beliefs we hold regarding ourselves. Frequently, we adopt wrong assumptions through a thought that has been repeated endlessly, usually due to false conclusions and incorrect interpretations. Richard Bach wrote in his beautiful story, 'Jonathan Livingston Seagull' that 'the worst lies are the ones we tell ourselves.' Just as eating the wrong foods shows a lack of love for the body, accepting a toxic relationship filled with abuse demonstrates a lack of self-love and low self-esteem and a call for help. These negative dynamics are not exclusive to partner relationships. Mistreating others, ignoring their feelings, and deceiving or lying to them is just as much a lack of self-love as receiving abuse. A person who loves himself would never consciously harm anyone. In a like manner, we mistreat ourselves when we allow our bosses, friends, or children to be disrespectful to us.

Accepting toxic love is rooted in the thinking that you are worthless and undeserving.

Unfortunately, we have seen how these subconscious beliefs attract similar people and thoughts. Thoughts create our future and our experiences. Beliefs attract thoughts of the same kind, and unknowingly, they also rule our decisions and emotions. For example, if you have a subconscious belief that you do not deserve love, your choices and their consequences will reflect this lie. You will not have healthy limits, and whether you want to or not, you will subconsciously agree to demeaning behaviors or situations dishonoring your Divine essence. Thoughts don't create reality as much as your silent master, the subconscious mind. Neglecting yourself and your body, eating unhealthy foods, sleeping less than what you need, overworking, going to extremes in sex, and abusing toxic substances like alcohol, tobacco, and drugs are the most evident signs of lack of self-love and self-respect.

How many times have we found ourselves in the same toxic relationship repeatedly because we felt comfortable; for example, a relationship with someone who abuses drugs or alcohol because unknowingly it reminded us of a parent? The root of this behavior might be hidden in our past.

Fearless love

When we live authentically, there is no need to deceive others by hiding who we are for fear of showing what we feel. In an entirely loving experience, we express our true feelings freely. There is coherence between our actions, our words, and our thoughts. The opposite happens when a relationship is unholy (meaning not whole or broken) when genuine feelings are motivated by manipulation and self-centeredness. The worst weapon in love is silence. We think we control by hiding our feelings as if holding back the information will give us an advantage over the relationship. But in reality, the only thing our silence accomplishes is to stop the flow of love, not only to the other person but also to ourselves since the other person can see through the silence.

One of the barriers to true love is avoiding intimacy at all costs to protect ourselves from rejection. Fear of intimacy can be disguised in many forms, including pride. The biggest fear human beings experience is rejection; that is, the fear of not being accepted. It can overshadow any other fear, even the fear of death itself. Therefore, we base most of our decisions to avoid rejection. To experience a total and honest relationship in love, we must overcome the fear of rejection. To be honest, real, open, kind, loving, and authentic is the best way to increase the flow of love in your life. You are truly vulnerable when you dare to love; when you risk opening your heart to another by dismantling your armor and removing the masks hiding who you really are.

Fearless love means expressing your feelings, relaxing your shoulders, looking straight into another's eyes, merely sharing a smile, and being willing to keep your pride from guiding your feelings. You must show yourself just as you are and express what you feel. Allow yourself to share when you are feeling afraid, uncomfortable, sad, or uncertain since you have a right to feel what you feel. Sharing what you feel with your partner is not a sign of weakness, but a sign of courage. Listening to what your partner is sharing about what he is feeling is also an act of courage.

Falling in love without 'the fall'

An unknown author came up with this wise quote: 'Nobody is perfect until you fall in love with them.' Healthy expectations and sensible boundaries have a place in our love lives, showing our self-love. Unrealistic expectations may carry the seed of disappointment. Nevertheless, we should have reasonable expectations of respect, commitment, authenticity, and honesty from the loved one. We deserve to receive love in the same proportion as we give it. In a toxic relationship, this balance is broken.

At the beginning of a toxic relationship, it is common to see a person create a filter that defuses and justifies many of the warning signs of the potential problems of another. If we become attached from the start, our fear of losing their love, together with the demands and expectations we place on others, can interfere with reason. Delaying a sexual relationship is always a good idea, not only because of morals but because it can lead to unhealthy attachments before we have used our reason. In the early stages of a toxic relationship, it is common to show an unconditional self, accepting all behaviors of the loved one. In this stage, we are not necessarily seeing the real person. Instead, we see a false portrait of what we believe that person could become. But the truth is: we cannot fall in love with a person's 'potential' to change. We see the red flags, yet we justify them. We hear the concerns of friends and family, yet we brush them aside. If we close our eyes to the truth, we will give away the keys to our hearts, worshipping the desired one and subconsciously adapting ourselves to be accepted and loved – some will even go to the extent of becoming martyrs. With time, we will see this person fall from the pedestal where we have placed them.

Idolatrous relationships can travel from one extreme of love straight to the bottom of hate, sometimes in a very short time. When this happens, we suddenly see the reality of their imperfections. We become resentful upon realizing that no one can give us what we have not been able to give ourselves. A crisis will follow with the added inconvenience of attachment, which is the experience of fearing the loss of what we erroneously thought to be the only source of our happiness. We conquer our fears when we understand that no one has control over our own power to love or to be happy unless we give them our consent.

The opposite is true in a healthy relationship, where we ideally meet halfway and see the other person for what they are and not for what we wished them to be. Thus, we can discern if the relationship is truly the best for us both. In fact, we experience true love, once we have traveled over the turbulent waters of romance and arrived safely on the calm shores of true love. True love is born when we grow beyond those unreliable first moments of falling in love when we may be blinded by illusion.

Authentic love reveals itself after transcending the short-lived mountains of passion, illusion, and hormones. Love matures when we can experience love with 'open eyes', as Jorge Bucay writes so well. The love that surpasses illusions reveals itself after the stage of passion ends; this love can travel through the rhythms of time and the ups and downs of life's seasons. We can overcome the monotony of the routine with the gifts of honesty, integrity, dedication, compassion, courtesy, sweetness, humor, and patience.

> *Mature love occurs when two souls unite so fully that each person's individuality shines brighter together than each would have if they had remained alone.*[22]

To reach a lasting love relationship, we must first fall in love with that which is timeless – the enduring values. If you fall in love with a body, the last name, power, a social standing, a bank account, or a profession, and those things change or end, then what you considered to be love will inevitably end with them. A love that is in constant growth, transforming, maturing, and deepening into the real essence of love itself,

---

[22] For more on the theory of mature love, read the work of Eric Fromm.

inevitably takes you into an actual merging of the souls. Everlasting love is not based on a feeling, but on a daily choice; this is the real definition of the word *commitment*.

Keeping your center

There is a fundamental law of polarity in the universe; in the physical world, everything is negative and positive, black and white, warm and cold, yin and yang. The secret is to live in balance – what Buddha called the middle way.

Life is a long battle to remain in the center; even the original Greek translation of the word sin, *hamartia*, means missing our target as in the sport of archery. Feeling off-center is the first symptom of imbalance in any area of our lives. It is essential to know how to see the positive and negative qualities in our partners and understand that even a positive quality may become a problem in the future. A typical example of this is when one of the members of the couple is too close to his parents. An admirable trait initially, however, it may jeopardize the couple's relationship, if taken to the extreme.

A couple's balance in the seven areas of the personal life portfolio – body and health, abundance, spirituality, service, love relationships, family, and true purpose – is helpful to create harmony. At times, new agreements need to be reached, and old ones revised. We have many pacts subconsciously sealed due to habit or routine that may need to be re-examined from time to time. Relationships are not static. It is also useful to learn to forgive and tolerate differences since we will never find a person without any defects. We are not without them ourselves.

True freedom in love

Freedom is letting go of the need to make others behave in a certain way. When someone fails to please us, we become disappointed. Only a person who is free from false expectations is capable of truly loving and being loved. If being angry and sad or happy and in love depended on others, we would be like ships adrift in the sea. Regardless of what anyone says or does against you, no one has the actual power to make you feel a certain way. Only you can choose what to accept, believe, and experience within yourself, be it positive or negative.

The opposite of freedom is attachment – the fear of losing something we believe is vital and irreplaceable for our survival. As the Buddha taught, attachment is the leading cause of suffering. Extreme detachment, however, could result in apathy and indifference, and this is just as toxic. Attachment and indifference are two sides of the same coin. Attachment, love, indifference, and hate are aspects of the same energy. If they had a temperature, hatred would be as cold as a frozen glacier and attachment would be as hot as the desert. True love, however, would be like the tepid breeze on a gentle day in spring.

We all have negative attachments to different things. Some people say that they are detached from love, yet they show attachment to money, obsessively working to avoid losing it. Others are detached from money yet are obsessive with their children; for example, mothers who live through their accomplishments. Some people are attached to fame, some to recognition; others are attached to their own ideals, or even feel sorry for themselves to the point of using persistent illness to secure the wrong kind of attention and sympathy from others. Other people are attached to resentment. Still others are attached to suffering, and the list goes on and on. We tend to be attached to whatever we have defined as an irreplaceable source of pleasure or safety, be it consciously or subconsciously.

Unhealthy attachments may compromise your ability to see things clearly, including the thought of being right. These attachments will lead us to justify everything to cling to whatever we feel is indispensable. On the contrary, healthy detachment, as Eastern philosophies teach, is being aware and remaining neutral. It is better to stand still when facing a challenge and proceed in a healthy and objective way.

Necessary bonds

There are healthy and necessary attachments in nature, such as the bond between mother and child. The same way a connection between a fawn and its mother can save the fawn's life in the forest, our connection with God is essential for our survival. Similar to the fawn's case, this bond will protect us from losing our way and falling victim to predators.

Healthy attachment is a voluntary commitment to recognizing real values, such as the value of life, a great love, another human being and his feelings, integrity, universal rights, and non-negotiable principles. Extreme detachment that is bordering on indifference is destructive not just in love but also in all other areas of life. Sociopaths are known for not being able to feel empathy. Humans cannot survive without healthy connections. True freedom in love is the result of knowing that nothing in this world is permanent, that we cannot hold on to anything for too long. Everything on this Earth is temporary and passing, including our own lives. Such is the nature of our physical world.

> *The only constant is change ... No one ever steps in the same river twice.*
>
> — Heraclitus, Greek philosopher

People also change; thus, attaching ourselves to the way someone was in the past is illogical. We cannot control the actions and choices of others, mainly when those changes are unexpected, such as a breakup or sudden changes in their behavior towards us. It does not make sense to depend on anything outside of ourselves since we cannot stop change. We can only choose how we respond in the face of the unforeseen events happening around us.

Healthy boundaries in love

True love rejoices in the presence of the mere existence and happiness of the other, but never at its own expense. It is also implied that the other loves himself and has self-dignity and self-respect. Punitive silence, physical or emotional abuse, lust, drug addiction, alcoholism, addictive gambling, deranged sex, self-centeredness, infidelity, dishonesty, humiliation, and lack of self-respect or respect for others are never negotiable. For this reason, it is accurate to state that some relationships may not last forever.

The religious belief of having to stay together forever despite mistreatment or lack of love is why some people stay in an abusive or loveless relationship. This is especially true of women. They may fear social disapproval, financial instability, or being left alone. Their fear may cause them to stay for the sake of the children or from social pressures. Couples who stay together based on guilt instead of love find other outlets, such as long hours at work, new interests, or even other relationships. Infidelity might happen for many reasons: loneliness, personal dissatisfaction, or fear of making decisions that go against society. It is well known that some describe their motivation for infidelity as a way to stay in the relationship.

In new relationships, things can be complicated; social media and unclear boundaries can also complicate relationships by opening doors to new conversations and fueling parallel love interests. It is possible to fall in love with another while in a relationship; nevertheless, love and fidelity go hand in hand with willpower and truth. Love is not a feeling; ultimately, it is a choice. In the case of the inevitable, we need to make new choices based on the bigger picture of the relationship instead of one event. If the relationship is worth keeping, we need to learn to forgive or rather ask for forgiveness ourselves. We are only human. That is why it is better to have a short but authentic relationship than a long marriage lacking commitment, love, or loyalty. Don't deprive yourself of the healthy opportunity to renegotiate less-than-ideal conditions to make your relationship work through time.

Some cases exist where couples agree to full freedom, and both members are free to enjoy the company of other outside partners. There are a significant number of fashionable arrangements that are not relationships but partnerships in pleasure. Pleasure and love are different. A relationship for pleasure alone hardly ever reaches its highest potential as authentic intimacy. More often than not, the relationship becomes a selfish transaction with convenient physical, emotional, or financial benefits. Inevitably, in the end, one or both members will be harmed.

> *True love looks for any means to share itself. Lust, on the other hand, only looks for ways to get love.*
>
> — Father Bernard Ligoria

When to let go

Partners in true love find two self-satisfied members, with no demands of or expectations from the other because their happiness is not dependent on the other. They are honest in what they can and cannot do for the other because everything in love isn't necessarily unconditional. Healthy limits exist because, contrary to some beliefs, not all is fair in love. No one should unconditionally accept actions against their principles. If you find that your partner offends you, ignores you, or simply makes you feel uncomfortable, search for the root. If there's abuse involved, get help. Violence is not only physical. Always listen to your intuition. If something does not feel right, it probably isn't.

Ask God to help you in letting go of a relationship that is no longer based on mutual respect. Love should not be treated casually; the age of instant gratification, choices, and fast dating has made love relationships easily replaceable. While love is not always going to last (*till death do you part*), we should do everything in our power to preserve a love relationship based on respect and true love. Nonetheless, if your partner decides, for example, to embrace an ideology extremely distant from yours (say, neo-Nazism), or if your partner chooses to live with another, then a lifetime commitment may not be a promise you need to keep.

True love does not try to hold on to someone who has chosen to move on. By holding on to anyone against their will, you are only keeping them from growing and finding their own happiness. At the same time, you deny yourself the right to do the same. We can't control how much anyone can love us or for how long, any more than we can stop the flow of a river.

Love never dies, but it can change and be transformed. For example, if the resentment caused by a breakup can be overcome, we might see how two lovers who have broken up can become friends, the same way two friends may end up as lovers. In the worst case, two lovers may also end up as enemies. Love and hate are extreme qualities of the same energy.

PRACTICE: OPENING YOURSELF TO TRUE LOVE

- **Identify your negative thoughts.** In your personal journal, begin identifying the negative beliefs you may hold regarding love relationships. Beliefs such as 'I do not deserve,' or 'All men/women are the same,' 'Love means sacrifices and suffering,' 'If I love someone, I'll lose my freedom,' or 'My only true love is ___________ (fill in the blank).' Those beliefs are silent sources of self-fulfilling prophecies of solitude. Make a list of all the other thoughts you hold about having a loving relationship. Observe all the past and present arguments that come up in your mind. Most negative thoughts are lessons learned from what you perceived while growing up, many from your parents and society. Once you identify the mistaken thought process, it begins to lose its power over you.

- **Ask God for your partner.** Simply ask God. Sometimes we think we want a partner, but deep inside, we are afraid to ask God because maybe our heart was wounded in the past, and we are not willing to risk pain again. If you are not ready to ask, you can always say the magic words: *God, I am afraid, but I trust you, and I am willing* ... Rest assured that when you are aligned to God's plan, He will show you your perfect partner at the right moment for both. Remember that your future partner must be available and ready as well.
- **Surrender your love relationships to God.** Sometimes we are not willing to surrender because we are attached to someone we loved in the past. Maybe we even made a silent promise to them. When we allow ourselves to be guided by the heart alone, we lose the ability to see all sides of a situation. If we cannot see clearly, we may choose the wrong partner, causing suffering to others as well as ourselves. Likewise, if we use our minds without our hearts, we might overlook the right person by letting appearances guide us. Surrender your loving relationships to God. I know this isn't always easy, but only He knows what is best for you.

When in doubt, surrender the person you love to the Will of God. As said in *A Course in Miracles*, we can symbolically place this person on the altar of God, where the Holy Spirit resides. If this person truly belongs with you, they will return to you completely renewed. In the case where that is not the best, in time, God will show you why it is necessary to let go of the relationship harmoniously and painlessly. We must be willing to listen.

- **Let go and let God.** Declare to God that you only desire His Will for you. Pray to God: *I do not want anything or anyone that you don't wish for me.* A brave declaration. Nevertheless, letting go is the only sensible solution. Allowing Divine Will to prevail over your own desires is fundamental. Hence, you will be able to see the situation objectively. Otherwise, your desire can interfere with your good and even justify intolerable behaviors. Much courage and detachment are needed for this declaration of trust. I assure you, if you let go, the truth will always be revealed, and there will be miracles in your relationships.

New roles in relationships

Significant changes are happening regarding our beliefs on what is the best model for a new love relationship. In the past, men were the sole providers. At the same time, women were expected to be submissive and without any ambitions other than to stay at home, which in many cases meant sacrificing their wishes to use their talents and search for their own purpose in life. Throughout history, men and women have had different roles in culture and society. During the war, men were on the battlefield, while the women worked outside of the home. Each stage has found men and women performing different roles. Sometimes the roles were necessary for survival, but traditionally, men acted the part of the dominant sex, resulting in women having to fight for their rights. Religion has been a principal sponsor of patriarchy and misogyny, but thankfully we are changing. For example, the Bahá'í Faith, a relatively new (mid-nineteenth century) but well-respected religion, originally from Persia (known as Iran today), promotes equality for women. This Bahá'í quote says it well:

> *Humanity is like a bird with its two wings – the one is male, the other female. Unless both wings are strong and impelled by some common force, the bird cannot fly heavenwards. According to the spirit of this age, women must advance and fulfill their mission in all departments of life, becoming equal to men. They must be on the same level as men and enjoy equal rights.*[23]

As per the new roles of the couple, each partner is truly committed to the other without losing their individuality in the relationship. They become one, but are not the same. Ideally, they are free of dependence, attachment, or fear of losing the relationship. Yet they still have a secure connection, where they are not detached or alienated from the other. Not to be confused with complete detachment where the arrangement in the relationship would be more like that of two separate strangers, joined only by convenience, need, or fear of loneliness.

---

[23] Abdu'l-Bahá at a meeting of the Women's Freedom League in London in January 1913.

Men, in general, have their own pressures about what is expected of them. When men are labeled as the sole providers and guardians of the social status by a partner, it becomes another source of increasing stress. A couple's agreements and values should be stated at the beginning of the relationship and discussed and revised as often as needed.

A relationship between two people is sacred. The human being you choose as your life partner is not an award, a trophy to show off, a possession, or someone to ward off loneliness. Your partner is not there to make you feel safe, to work as your servant, or to comply with society's expectations. This relationship is the union of two conscious, independent, and authentic human beings in complete integrity. Two people choose to unite with a shared or individual goal in love, spiritual growth, fulfillment, service, or enjoyment of life – sometimes helping others with their individual or shared talents.

In the end, all longing for unconditional love is nothing other than a reflection of our desire to become one with our source. Much like a baby longs for the mother's embrace, we all long to return to the Great Universal Mother's embrace. On this Earth, a resemblance to this oneness can also be experienced within a healthy loving relationship.

8

YOUR FAMILY

THE FAMILY – NO MATTER HOW THE MEMBERS IDENTIFY themselves – defines our values and continues to be the first stepping-stone towards well-being and contentment in our society. Whether it is a family of two or one of twenty, a family with a strong support structure of love and acceptance becomes the most significant advantage for an individual's emotional health. There are many variations of being a family. All families are valid because they reflect the realities of our society in the current state of evolution. They demonstrate how the paradigm of what a family should look like changes with time and context. For example, there are single mothers as well as single fathers. Another reality is that the new family does not necessarily have to include just a man and a woman. The rights of all families must be protected regardless of our personal beliefs or religion. Love is love. The real problem arises when people try to conform to the norms that society expects them to follow and suffer when they can't. When we truly learn to value both ourselves and others, no matter our gender or our choices, we will live as beings with integrity who do not need to conform to others' expectations for their approval.

In the past, families worked together for the common good of the village. But in recent times, most of us only consider tending to our immediate family members' needs exclusively.

We have forgotten about the words 'I was a stranger, and you welcomed me ...'[24] and anyone outside of our immediate family circle is considered a stranger. A time will come when there will be a universal family, meaning that everyone on the planet will be regarded as part of one's own family.

A new man and a new woman

The degree of evolution in a nation can be measured by the equal rights and choices granted to women. It is a fact that women were considered inferior, mostly because of poor interpretation of religious scriptures and the story of creation. This archaic model continues to justify inequality and the abuse of women. It still produces women filled with fears and guilt when they follow the voice of their hearts. Many are subject to abuse and mistreatment from their male partners who continue to have financial and emotional control over them. Laws that protect the equal rights of women, including equal pay, still fail to be ratified in most countries. The new woman has a leadership role in the present and future generations. Women now follow their intuition and increasingly participate in public life as they balance their natural woman-mother responsibilities,

---

[24] Matthew 25:35

which does not mean that women will become the *new man*. Each has its own nature to honor.

Sometimes what women see as rights can become a disadvantage when there is a conflict between her wishes to advance her career and stay home as a mother. In these times of financial challenge, women contributing to the family income is often a necessity. Poor mothers often don't have the choice to stay at home with their children. However, some progressive countries protect women financially so that they can stay at home longer with their children.[25] Ideally, mothers should be able to stay with their children during their early years. Educator Maria Montessori said that children absorb everything from their environment before age six. Fortunately, in our era, there are many options available to work from home or to find a job with a flexible schedule. I was lucky to be able to stay at home and educate my daughter during her first years. It was my preferred alternative. Of course, mothers who have no choice or who choose to work while raising their children are also loved and admired by their sons and daughters. Challenges arise for us as women when there is a conflict between what we 'want' to do and what we 'think' we should do according to our gender. It is not uncommon to see some women feeling guilty about working outside the

---

[25] The UN's children's agency (UNICEF) looked at the duration of fully paid parental leave for mothers and fathers and the availability of childcare for young children in thirty-one European countries in 2016. Estonia, Portugal, Germany, Denmark, Slovenia, Luxembourg, and France were among the top ten. See 'Nordic Countries Best for Young Families, Germany among Top 10 – UNICEF Report,' 13 June 2019, https://www.dw.com/en/nordic-countries-best-for-young-families-germany-among-top-10-unicef-report/a-49169343.

home and others feeling equally guilty when they choose to be stay-at-home mothers. Whether she decides to work inside or outside the home, she is always contributing to society. In the case of a woman who can and wishes to stay at home, she should be supported to do so. Women's choices must be honored. There is a season for everything, a time for child-rearing and a time to offer your talents to the world. What is important is to honor the will of the woman. I find that, when it comes to career and family, women are internally divided. We are seeing a trend where women are extremely conflicted by the world, so much that many are opting for either postponing or not having children at all. In many developed countries, the birth rate is at an all-time low, either because of political reasons, financial considerations, or climate concerns. I was hesitant to have a child and didn't become a mother until later in life. To me, becoming a mother was the best decision of my life. Each woman should honor her needs in the different stages of her life and find her balance, which only she can do for herself. Otherwise, she will not be able to enjoy either roles. There is a perfect moment for everything; it is a matter of honoring and identifying your inner needs.

This inner search becomes successful only through silence, meditation, and communion with God. You might be able to have it all, but you will have to decide if it can be all at the same time.

Raising your child

It is interesting to note that another word for upbringing is also 'raising'. Our arms were created to 'raise' our children above all the challenges of this world.

As infants, we devote ourselves to just *being*. In our first years, our only job is to express our authentic selves. When children are born, they experience the world as pure love, living in an eternal present with no consciousness of separation. There are no worries because, in a healthy environment, love is a given freely. Infants naturally know that they are part of The All. Infants live and are nurtured by their unity with their mother.

Birth is natural, yet it is frequently treated as a medical emergency or a disease. Medical facilities inadvertently interfere with the natural bonding process of mother and baby because of a lack of awareness. The tiny body isn't just a handful of involuntary reflexes, but a sentient, crying human with memory. The medical staff forgets that the newborn is a full-blown soul who has arrived to experience his mission on Earth.

Replacing loving arms with swings and a face-to-face conversation with screen time – these and other new inventions cannot substitute human touch. Humans are the most sophisticated creation on the planet and are perfect. Let's not compromise human development by tampering with a perfect mechanism that was specially designed by God. Soon after my daughter's birth, I served on the Baby-Friendly USA Hospital board of directors and collaborated with this beautiful UNICEF initiative for many years. At that time, my eyes were opened by meeting scientific researchers who worked on reforming maternity care, including the late Dr. Marshall Klaus, who, together with his wife Phyllis, founded DONA International, the first doula[26] initiative. Dr. Klaus also presented research on the benefits of skin-to-skin contact, which is now part of UNICEF/WHO Ten Steps to Successful Breastfeeding hospital protocols. Promoting a healthy birthing experience includes giving birth without unnecessary interventions and avoiding separation from the baby while providing love, time, and support to the mother safely and, above all, with reverence. From the work of these researchers and others, I learned that to ensure humans' healthy survival, we urgently need to return to the recommended natural options and avoid unnecessary practices that interfere with the natural process of bonding.[27] Dr. Klaus carried out studies demonstrating to the medical community the obvious advantages of following the wisdom of nature. For example, it is important not to separate mother and child. If possible, the baby and mother should be allowed full skin-to-skin contact during the first hour after birth, when the chemical and spiritual affective bond is heightened through the baby's senses.

The bottle was only introduced to humanity after the 19th century, and it became the norm for generations. Breastfeeding, however, is the most beautiful experience

---

[26] 'Doula' in Greek means a 'woman's servant'. A trained professional who provides continuous physical, emotional, and informational support to a mother before, during, and shortly after childbirth to help her achieve the healthiest, most satisfying experience possible. See https://www.dona.org/what-is-a-doula/.

[27] For more information about the steps under the UNICEF Baby Friendly Hospital initiative, visit https://www.unicef.org/nutrition/files/BFHI_Case_Studies_FINAL.pdf.

of all, since it consists of nurturing the baby in all ways. It is a natural design. The world's health goal is to favor a natural choice over commercialization, returning to our natural origins.

Some clinical and psychological conditions can prevent or make it difficult for mothers to breastfeed, including some who have been sexually abused. However, many times, a mother's inability to breastfeed is caused by medical mismanagement, lack of knowledgeable personnel, no training, wrong information, or formula marketing. In days of climate change and natural disasters, we can consider how breastfeeding mothers would benefit in a natural emergency, even possibly as a means of survival for both their babies and themselves since they would always have a food supply. Even in a state of malnutrition, a breastfeeding woman could continue feeding her baby; it is part of her nature. The survival of the species is a priority. However, breastfeeding is a mother's choice; it should be enough for her medical team to present scientific evidence. Once she has decided not to breastfeed, for whatever reason, the use of guilt is not necessary.

Up until age seven, children live in a dream world, fully connected to their Divine essence. They see the world through their imagination. It is a mistake to interrupt this state of imagination to bring the child into the adult reality of facts and even intellectually strenuous efforts before his time. Many experts are now confirming what holistic child educators stated a century ago. We seem to be in a hurry to end childhood. Earlier is not always better. Research has shown that children benefit from and prefer simple toys, like stones, blocks, wood or fabric pieces, and craft dolls that they can infuse with their images.[28] Children's imaginations will take care of the rest; for example, a simple piece of fabric turned into a costume or a piece of wood transformed into a ship can become the child's favorite toy. We should also allow them to observe and immerse themselves in nature without rational explanations, competition, or interruptions. Simply allow them to experiment and discover their new environment by themselves as guided by their curiosity. It is this simple: we should let kids be kids.

Perhaps imagination is only intelligence having fun.

— Albert Einstein

Loving guidance

In her book *Discipline with Love*, author and friend Rosa Barocio, cautions parents about avoiding discipline altogether. Parents who do not use discipline may be reacting to experiences with their parents, who perhaps treated them too harshly during childhood. Other parents just fear being rejected by their children and resort to become their child's best friend. Some overcompensate as they feel guilty about their absence.

It is a mistake to be either a permissive or an excessive disciplinarian. Corporal punishment leaves scars beyond the body. Nevertheless, we should never lose sight of

---

[28] 'Simple Retro Toys May Be Better For Children Than Fancy Electronic Toys,' ScienceDaily (ScienceDaily, 26 November 2007), https://www.sciencedaily.com/releases/2007/11/071123204938.htm.

teaching children the right path and expecting respect, cooperation, and order, as they follow our house rules. Children should be the object of our attention and love. Still, it is also important not to give in to their every wish, for this creates egocentric, attention-addicted adults who expect instant gratification and are unable to abide by rules or manage their temperament – quite the opposite of what we are striving for. Children should be an integral part of the family, but not the unbalanced, central focus of unhealthy conceited attention. Extremes are not desirable, neither an excess of attention nor a complete lack of it.

Our loved ones

If at any time you feel different from the rest of your family, if sometimes you seriously think that you were switched at birth, you are not alone. Regardless of whether you were born with a family or without one, without a mother or a father, or with a grandmother who raised you, most of what you think about yourself developed from that environment, including your purpose and its lessons. There is no doubt that we can always learn from even less-than-ideal family situations. It is not a mistake. We must accept our beginnings. We come to this Earth in groups of souls, and we need to come to terms with our experience and be grateful for the family we received.

We always have a choice. It is also important to realize that any sort of permanent mistreatment is unacceptable; guilt sometimes drives us to erroneous decisions regarding our family. To honor your father and mother means acknowledging a pact of responsibility and respect, which is different from accepting everything they say as the truth.

You owe your family respect and loyalty, but you do not have to follow unsound beliefs or repeat negative patterns, habits, or abuses. If you are in such a situation, then you will, at some point, have to spread your wings and make your own decisions. Parents have the guiding role up till the age of twenty-one. After that, the relationship and the guidance will continue, but with much respect to the offspring and their independence.

Ideally, a family should stay close, even if miles apart. Your family should be your safe harbor and your reference, as long as there is respect on both sides. Nowadays, there are many types of families, and we cannot be attached to an ideal image. What truly matters is being responsible and knowing how to respond to our family situation. We are under the impression that other people's families are ideal, but that is far from true. Appearances and social media are deceiving. Don't get fixed on having a perfect family.

Most of your beliefs – negative and positive ones – about yourself, others, and life, in general, were formed under the influence of your family. Taking some time to review them is of vital importance. Nevertheless, make sure that you show tolerance, forgiveness, and respect towards your family's different opinions. Most probably, there are members of your family with beliefs and customs different from yours. That is normal and enriching. Simply accept this difference without having to assume the same views as your own or without needing to change others' beliefs. It is also very probable that someone in the heart of your family taught you or inspired the very qualities you needed for your purpose. Maybe your uncle inspired you to become a musician, or perhaps your grandmother taught you to become a painter. If you are a surgeon, you probably inherited your father's miracle-working hands. In the past, professions were passed down from one generation to another; thus, producing a higher quality, more knowledgeable professional with each new generation. Sadly, some may automatically reject the family craft or business only because they want to prove they can succeed for themselves. Often, we can't see the blessings of our family because we take them for granted, or because their particular way of being does not conform with what success should look like.

The opposite can also be the case when a well-intentioned fatherly opinion regarding what path you should take sends you walking along the way of the wrong profession throughout your lifetime. Maybe you wanted to work with children and ended up as an attorney, or you might end managing your dad's business because it was your dad's dream, but it isn't yours. We must remember that we are free and that it is never too late to resume the path of our authentic dreams.

Make peace with your family. If you have past resentments and have drifted away from your family, it is time to make amends. Most people have issues pending with family members. Isn't it time to forgive your father for having abandoned your mother decades ago? Isn't it time to stop penalizing your relative with such indifference for whatever happened years ago? Despite the mistake a family member may have made, it is essential to realize that people do the best they can with the tools they have at that moment, according to their state of consciousness and baggage. Take time to find out more about this failing relative's childhood, and you may find yourself understanding his behavior, unacceptable as it was. For help in letting go of a traumatic situation involving a relative, I recommend using the forgiveness technique described later in this book.

Friends, companions for our seasons

Life chooses our family, but friends are the family we choose for ourselves. Some are our friends for a lifetime, and some for only a season. They usually appear in different places and times to help us on our path. Sometimes we may need to assist them through a transition or maybe as part of a mutual life project.

Some friends come along to guide us, while others are there to test us. Some show up to teach us about giving; others to show us about receiving. Some arrive to teach us trust, and still others come to teach us how to discern. Some friends teach us to forgive and others teach us to forgive ourselves. Some very dear friends move on to different learning stages, or they are no longer connected to our vision or values. Understandably, people change, and sometimes we must learn to let them go. True friends are few and far between, as the saying goes. Many times, we confuse friends with business associates or contacts; nevertheless, relationships should always be authentic. A business friendship that is not authentic will end when the transaction is finished.

There are also friends beyond friendship – a sort of twin flame with whom we may have made a pact while in Heaven. Perhaps we said something like, 'Remember me whenever we meet on Earth.' These friends may be loved even more than we love our own family. They are not common, but with them, we feel free to share and support each other. Some may help us while living, and others will help us while dying. This sort of friendship is beyond special and belongs to our soul group. They may guide us to our purpose during a specific time; they help us grow and keep our eyes on the horizon.

Other friends are living parallel lives similar to ours. When someone is going through the same experience, either surviving cancer or losing a loved one, the lessons that are shared are more comfortable to endure. It is not unusual to meet a new friend after a divorce or another extreme situation. They might also appear at the birth of a child. Or meet at a time of loss, and their only purpose is to share the time and the experience. Sometimes they stay for a long time, and sometimes their company may be brief; nonetheless, they always show up at the right moment. Of course, some friends end up as love relationships since friendship is the prelude to a great love.

I cannot end this section of friends without mentioning our dear pets – soul companions who sometimes even mirror our healing and our pain. They are angels sent to us. Who is more unconditional than our pets? While translating this book, I lost one of my cats, a friend for seventeen years, and I can assure you, he was family. He is survived by a white Persian. Over many years, they have been my loyal companions in good times and bad. They have souls, and we will meet them again in Heaven.

Whenever you meet someone new, instead of asking what he or she does for a living, ask about their dreams and find out what both of you have in common. Remember, no encounter is coincidental.

Every meeting we have is a scheduled appointment.

— Jorge Luis Borges

Reconnecting with friends

While most of us are always busy, there is no doubt that we must take time each day to be grateful for our friends. Call and visit those who are close by and tell them that you love them. Send an email or a handwritten card to those far away, telling them of their importance in your life despite the distance. For those who have passed away, you can light a candle and send them a prayer. If you have a spiritual debt pending, contact the friend you may have mistreated and let go of past resentments. The saddest thing, and this has happened to me, is to delay contacting a friend assuming they will be there forever, only to find out one day, it is too late. Use whatever method you choose, either by phone, postal mail, or email, and let the other person know you love them. If there's any pending debt with someone who has passed away, in your mind, say that it has been canceled and then let them go. You will feel better and lighter once this is done.

9

YOUR TRUE PURPOSE

We all have a gift to give

WE USUALLY CATCH A GLIMPSE OF OUR PURPOSE EARLY IN life – say, at the age of four or five. It probably involved a favorite activity of ours that filled those around us and ourselves with joy. A wise man once told me that children also receive a strong revelation of their true mission in life around age twelve. At this early age, Jesus went missing and was found preaching to the elders at the temple, revealing his gift as a teacher of teachers. A parent's job is to be aware of these gifts and provide their children with the tools to develop their talents. We are not born prodigious; every skill needs to be honed. However, some parents themselves become the most significant obstacle by paying more attention to what society expects of the child than to his natural talents. Can you imagine what would have happened if Mozart's father had neglected his son's musical abilities?

When I was young, I loved drawing dresses for my girlfriends. As an adult, I studied for a career I did not enjoy until I listened to my heart and left my hometown in Puerto Rico to go to New York to study design. Fashion merchandising became my career of choice for a season of my life. It felt as if my mission was to inspire others through beauty. It was not by chance that I met my dear teacher Dada Vaswani, through friends from the business – since our careers are only an excuse for relationships and learning. Later on, after pursuing my career in fashion, I began to organize conferences for motivators and teachers on spirituality. That particular interest started as a young girl when I discovered the spiritual texts, my grandmother zealously kept. Today I still have the same urge to learn more about why things work the way they do, together with my desire to share what I learn with others. My purpose continues to be the same, whether as a fashion designer, a writer, a motivational speaker, or an event organizer. My purpose is to share beauty, find meaning, and inspire personal and social change. What is yours?

We all have experiences in our lives that can become the treasure map that leads us towards our true purpose. These revealing experiences may occur at any time, as a child or in adulthood. They inspire us to grow, find answers to our questions, and heal by helping others through the lessons we learned.

One of the experiences that marked my life happened in my adolescence while trying to escape from a dysfunctional home. The fear, desperation, and frustration I went through also led me to discover my own purpose. The fact that I was able to find my purpose and peace using the tools I share in this book, despite being born in the middle of unfavorable circumstances, is my greatest satisfaction. Helping others find their own path is my primary motivation.

The seasons and your purpose

The soul's journey towards its purpose is not always a straight line – it can be filled with pauses, detours, restarts, and delays along the way. Nothing stays the same, even if we can't perceive the difference. When a season passes, it always leaves the gift of change before we move on to the next. Each new season brings the dawn of a new perspective. The purpose of the journey lies in the discovery of new horizons, not in the arrival at a safe harbor.

If we understood the wisdom of nature, we would also trust that the same intelligence that gave the scent to the flower will also give us the tools for our purpose. The purpose of the gardenia is to bring joy through its beauty and perfume. The flower that lacks a bright color might be compensated with an intoxicating fragrance. We can't force our purpose; it is the natural expression of our being. We cannot become someone we are not, but we can become the person we are meant to be. Everything exists in perfect harmony.

Our gift is the same, but its expression may change

Our lives have many seasons, and we may have different professions, yet the essence of our purpose will remain the same. A good friend of mine wrote music and was a well-known TV producer until the age of forty. After forty, he studied psychology, finished his doctorate, and became a renowned self-help author in Puerto Rico. His name is Dr. Alfred D. Herger, author of *Yo Voy a Mí (I Believe in Me)*. His eagerness to motivate and inspire others was always the same, but the expression of his purpose changed with his life experience.

I had a career in fashion until age thirty-six; it coincided with the end of a nine-year cycle. Once my daughter was born, I decided to spend her first years at home, dedicating all of my time to being with her – a decision I do not regret. After being a lifelong feminist and delaying motherhood in favor of my career, I discovered my love for children. I became an active advocate for mothers' and children's rights, yet another channel to express my talent for bringing awareness.

The key to success is to be flexible and reinvent oneself when the season calls for a pause or a change of direction. There's no escaping the lessons of growth. Unfinished business of one season will eventually meet us again at a later time. However, lingering in a season beyond its time is not desirable. It is common these days to see people over thirty living an eternal adolescence. Avoiding each cycle's responsibilities unnecessarily stretches the time allotted to complete it, creating physical and psychological imbalances. As the saying goes: 'There is a time and place for everything.'

Our purpose in the world

The common good is our main purpose, no matter what our gifts are. Love and compassion are the common denominators to build a fair society. Groups that use their talents solely for the personal gain, well-being, and material satisfaction of a few, whether religious or for-profit companies are destined to become a part of the past. Hidden agendas cannot prosper under the disguise of altruism, even with the help of costly marketing and advertising campaigns. No one can fool the Divine

Intelligence for long since the universe eventually will give us the bill for our debts.

Working with integrity while providing our gifts to the planet is the difference between building and destroying, offering hope and breeding despair, bringing peace and promoting hate, giving life and destroying with death. For example, an evident lack of integrity is seen in tobacco companies that target young women in advertisements by portraying a beautiful slim woman as an ideal of independence and beauty. Is there anyone unaware of the fact that smoking is one of the leading causes of cancer?

We are as responsible for what we know, as we are for what we don't want to know. Universal laws, just as with the laws of physics, are impartial – every cause has an effect, every effect has a cause, and each result has its own consequences. The trail left by consequences can linger for a long time after the fact. It may be positive or negative and may affect a wide or narrow range of people, time, and space.

> *Ignorance of the law does not exempt us from its consequences.*

The quality of every result will depend on the intent behind the original act or cause. Therefore, we must stop to consider all the consequences before making every choice. Everything bears its own fruit. The temptation of instant gratification can blind our ability to see the future. Harmful advertising will bring forth a stream of death and destruction, with long-term negative consequences affecting future generations as well.

A YOUNG MAN WITH THE WRONG PURPOSE

Some years ago, I met a very peculiar young man on a flight from Miami. He was dressed in flashy clothes and jewelry, yet he did not seem happy or at ease. During our conversation, he couldn't explain what he did for a living and, among other suspicious things, mentioned that he admired the drug dealers in his neighborhood because they 'helped people out more than politicians.' However, I noticed that his expression changed when he showed me a picture of his small boy, stating that his son was the most important person in his life. A father with the wrong purpose will only pass on a dark legacy to his offspring. As we left the plane, I invoked all the angels to guide and protect his family, and I felt that our conversation made a difference.

Anyone who is partaking in a dark business, legal or not, will know on a subconscious level that promoting merchandise or causes that are harmful to the lives of thousands of youngsters and their families, will have spiritual consequences. His soul will also know that, according to the law of cause and effect or karma, if he doesn't change direction, at some point, he will probably have to shed tears for each death he has caused. Life will show him, even if financially successful, that no one can get rich at the expense of the unhappiness of others. The talent of a drug dealer is the same as that of a good merchandiser. He could just as well use the same gift to market something worthwhile for humanity. However, some prefer to take the easy road.

Unethical economics

A new wave of consciousness is awakening humanity to the fact that we can no longer tolerate selfishness and lack of integrity in businesses. It may appear that some cannot lose while growing with all the advantages and zero consequences. Nevertheless, the universe has a way of moving us in the direction of a new and better way of life.

One case in point is the banking industry. The new economics will show families how to manage money matters and contribute to the sustainable development of the planet, instead of encouraging their debt. In an ideal world, the new bank will also become a mentor to countless companies, big and small, to support the good of humanity. We all need to work together towards this vision.

The law of compensation

In some countries, we see how the cycle of loss will eventually interrupt a growing economy, which could be explained as part of the natural cycles and the law of compensation at work. This law, made popular in an essay by Ralph Waldo Emerson, notes that nothing is wasted; everything is used for the good of all. For example, since the Divine plan needs you, if you are working at a job where your purpose, talents, and energy are not valued or for the good of all, the great Wisdom will allow you to advance towards your ideal place. In this case, losing can be winning. Your talents and purpose are essential. Search within, and you will find the change is a blessing.

The coronavirus pandemic of 2020 took us on an unintended dive within ourselves. At the same time, the

Earth took a needed pause from the contamination that results from our unhealthy choices of energy consumption. The disease affected millions, collapsing our lungs, which, according to Ayurveda, represents the center of our being and the fourth chakra, also called Anahata, which means 'unhurt' in Sanskrit – associated with calmness and serenity when in balance. Unsurprisingly this center, which also governs the lungs, represents the heart. The Chakra of the Heart, according to Hindu tradition, balances our emotions of love and also rules anger, jealousy, fear, and hate. In the middle of the pandemic and protests that sparked around the world, decrying racism and the killing of George Lloyd in the US – the words that were adopted as a symbol of oppression were his last words, 'I can't breathe.'

Rampant negative emotions have separated us from our spiritual oxygen, which is the love of God. The soul of the Earth cannot breathe asphyxiated by all the physical and emotional pollution we are harboring.

The crises of today are simply the world's attempts to regain its balance. It is impossible to withdraw from the Earth's bank account indefinitely without finding one day that the treasury is empty. Abusing the Earth's resources will only contribute to a lifeless future, as wasting our personal energy without refueling it, will only bring illness. The same holds true for our spirit. If we fail to nurture our souls with good thoughts, prayers, meditation, nature, and service, it will eventually fall into spiritual bankruptcy.

> *For every action, there is an equal and opposite reaction.*
>
> — Isaac Newton

If you have lost something recently, stay still and do not worry: 'Be still and know that I am God.'[29] Even if we can't see the reason for a loss, the pendulum of balance is quietly moving in a better direction. You will always be protected if you walk with God. Remember that according to this law of balance, you may find that those who have suffered will experience an unexpected joy, those who have lost a business will gain time with their grandchildren, or those who have lost a dear one may likely receive news of a birth.

Blessed are they who mourn, for they shall be comforted.

— The Beatitudes

What would happen if one of the cells in your body decided to work only for itself with complete disregard for the rest of the body? If the cell, by sheer selfishness, chose not to share its energy or its mission, it would quickly become a destructive or cancerous cell. The same happens when people act only to benefit themselves. When we steal money, we are stealing from ourselves. If we destroy the planet, we destroy our own house, and by not paying our employees a fair salary, we are depleting ourselves. If you purchase a counterfeit item or shop in an unfair market, you are only participating in the darkness and deceiving yourself. The universe's raw materials are exclusive to no one. Ultimately, the universe works to integrate its energy for the highest good. When you hold back from using your talent, you are also taking away the opportunity from others to enjoy your gift. You are similar to the small

[29] Psalm 46:10

cell, apparently insignificant but unique in its mission. Remember, the 'all' cannot be the 'The All' without your part. Do not worry. Although life is in constant change, we never lose something without being duly compensated by God. That is the law.

It is a mistake to think that finding our purpose will always bring fame, recognition, and material success. We have the right to a reward; nevertheless, that should not be our primary goal in life. If that is our only goal, then emptiness and dissatisfaction will remain regardless of all our success.

Undoubtedly, the highest purpose we can have is to awaken to the plan God has for us – by connecting to His Will. Elevating our thoughts to make a conscious connection with His plan is the only way to find our inner purpose. Most people live backwards: they want to *have*, in order to *do*, to be able to *be*. The opposite is true. First, you must learn to *be* and to *do*, in order to have the corresponding results.

Your real purpose feels different. Finding your purpose will bring immense joy when we share it with others as a service. But if you miss giving your talent, you will feel emptiness and dissatisfaction. A truly fulfilling life that flows with real success is the result of offering your gift as a service to others.

Now more than ever, the world needs you. Don't waste your talents watching the news on TV or staying glued to social media. Don't complain about the government or a job you dislike.

Resolve to make a difference. Neutralize that sense of dissatisfaction by practicing loving purposeful action.

Silence, meditation, time alone in nature, questioning, and observing yourself, together with active reflection, will give you clues on how to use your talents to help others. Most importantly, ask God daily how you may best serve Him and others.

It is not as important what you do – working as a waiter, a president, or a doctor – what matters is you do everything with love and excellence. The value of our purpose is to be grateful for each moment we give, never as a duty or for your selfish benefit or recognition. The world has been blessed with the gifts and talents of many invisible hands that have never been acknowledged; they all share the common goal of quietly serving with love. God sees you.

How to discover your purpose

Some scholars state that we reach full use of our reason at twenty-one. Unfortunately, other sages affirm that a veil may fall over our real mission at that same age. Maybe this is why adolescents are so confused, searching for their *authentic Self* everywhere. If we do not find our purpose in life, then our mid-forties or fifties may meet us with a profound identity crisis. Trying to find our true meaning during adulthood may turn into a virtual archaeological expedition trying to find clues, among forgotten fossils in our lives that will reveal traces of our original purpose.

A spiritual teacher once said that if you feel you must fix the world, it is probably not your real purpose, because the purpose is never manifested as a duty, but as an inexplicable need to share your talents and interests.

How to find your north

Birds know that they must migrate to avoid freezing or dying in the cold of winter. Penguins and whales swim through a long and challenging journey to a specific location every year to find their mates. We human beings hardly ever have a clear idea of which path to take in our lives. Animals have instinct, a sort of ingrained compass. When the time comes to move, it becomes inevitable. The instinct to them is greater than any emotion. Animals in nature are simply connected to God's plan. What are we connected to? Do we still have instincts, or are our senses completely impaired?

Our inner voice speaks clearly to us during our first years of life, but throughout the years, people around us, unknowingly silence that voice with their doubts and ideas. We have heard the story countless times: a young man or woman dreams of becoming a painter, writer, or acrobat, only to hear from others that artists die of hunger and that a better career would be one where a good job and salary is assured. Likewise, many times when you enjoy what you do, society labels your occupation as a pastime and makes you doubt yourself. The media may also confuse the direction of your true purpose by showing erroneous images of what is expected from successful people. For many of us, finding our path seems to happen by sheer luck or pure coincidence. But when we look closely, all the erroneous or twisted roads of our journey finally took us to our rightful destiny.

A LIFE OF MEANING

What would a life of meaning look like to you? Many researchers have been curious to learn how the people of Okinawa in Japan maintain the highest rate of longevity and the number of centenarians in the world. Okinawa, an island that lost close to 200,000 soldiers in World War II, still is well known for its hospitality, health, community, and joy of life. There are distinct factors that contribute to their overall health, including diet, good habits, rituals, and tropical weather. However, the main secret of Okinawans is that they've found *the reason to wake up in the morning;* in other words, they have found their *ikigai.*

In Japanese, the word 'ikigai' is made of two characters, one means 'life', and the other means 'to be worthwhile'. According to Dan Buettner, a National Geographic fellow and explorer who coined the term 'blue zones' and researched these areas (places where people live longer and with fewer cases of common diseases), Okinawans don't have a word for retirement. Dan arrived at this conclusion: 'People with purpose live longer, sleep better, and are healthier.'[30]

30 Quoted by Brianna Wiest, in 'Ikigai Is The Japanese Method Of Determining Whether Or Not Your Work Will Fulfill You," Forbes (Forbes Magazine, 21 March 2019), https://www.forbes.com/sites/briannawiest/2019/03/19/ikagi-is-the-japanese-method-of-determining-whether-or-not-your-work-will-fulfill-you/?sh=1a92d1a033fe.

PRACTICE: HOW TO LIVE YOUR PURPOSE

Here are some questions that can serve as guidelines towards your purpose:

- What are the things you do better than most and without much effort?
- What do people look to you for?
- What are your areas of expertise, even though they are not your main job?
- What are you extremely organized in?
- What did you enjoy doing as a child?
- What activities can you spend hours doing without taking notice of the time?
- What work would you do, even without pay?
- What experience marked your life as an adult or as a child?
- What would you do if you had all the time and money in the world?
- What would you do if you had a chance at another life at a place where no one knew your past?
- What would you do if you had only five years to live?

PART III

THE ORDER OF THINGS

IF WE TRAVEL TO A NEW COUNTRY, ASIDE FROM ROADMAPS, the first step is to learn the ways of this foreign place. The same happens on our planet. There are fundamental laws that we need to learn before filling out our 'job application' – in the form of our purpose. In this section, we will learn to recognize the order of things. One of the fundamental laws, known as 'as above, so below', describes a correlation between different life forms.

This truth is at the core of the laws of the universe and also applies to humans. The cycles of the planets affect us, just as the moon cycle affects the tides and our emotions. We have been studying the stars for centuries, trying to explain the timing of cosmic and personal events. According to Chinese medicine, our body is ruled by an established order with a specific schedule for its different functions. In the same way, the biological clock determines sleeping hours and mealtimes. Humans and animals are highly sensitive to any alterations in their life rhythm. These interruptions will immediately create imbalances and a gap between our natural cycles. Modifications in the natural rhythms may happen under stressful situations, like excessive studying or working, or when traveling to faraway places in a different time zone, bringing forth all sorts of disruptions.

Our heart also has its rhythm and cycles. Strong emotions may create severe arrhythmia and provoke an imbalance between its cycle and rhythm. In women, it has been evidenced that intense emotions may push them off their feminine rhythm and 28-day cycles. When a woman is upset, her menstrual cycle could be delayed – start before it is expected or stop altogether. Ayurveda, an ancient Hindu science, believes that if a man can control his breathing cycles, he may also control his life cycle and reach longevity.

The truth is that everything occurs in perfect mathematical order, almost predictably so. There are predictable cycles in nature as well as in finances, cultures, and the cosmos. The laws of synchronicity and coincidence are, in reality, natural events yet to be understood by humankind. Absolute predictions are impossible, like those of the much-discussed end of time. However, we have the power to collectively influence the final results of our future reality, since its outcome will vary depending on the collective algorithms of our thoughts, choices, and intentions, whether they are based on the ego or following God's order.

10

SEASONS OF THE SOUL

DOES THE SOUL GROW THROUGHOUT THE SEASONS THE same way that the body does? Does it transform through a life that is in constant change? Can we be in tune with our seasons? Yes, if we make a conscious effort to observe our lives. There is a part of the soul that is unchanging – but remember that the soul is also the sum of all our experiences. The seasons of the soul do not end in closed circles, but as open spirals – when one cycle ends, a new one immediately begins, taking us deeper into the previous lesson. There are no appointed arrival times on the spirals of life. We may feel frustrated after we promise ourselves that we have learned our lesson, only to find ourselves relapsing. Each time, however, the same lesson will be experienced at a deeper level and with a different set of tools. Our patient, compassionate soul will always give us another opportunity to learn the lesson at a deeper level of consciousness. We travel through the seasons at our own pace. Some people may seem to live in one eternal season, while others appear to be sailing through many. Some travel fast like an impatient child, and others stay in one season like an eternal elder. Still, others fight change, like an adolescent rebel. Ages may vary, but the rhythm of the universe does not. It breathes in and out, expanding and contracting, dying and rebirthing, sleeping and wakening to the constant compass of time.

Our lives and the universe evolve in a similar pattern of breathing in and breathing out. All creation is born as an idea, or as Genesis teaches, as the Logos, which means 'thought'. Then there's the material birth, followed by growth until we reach a peak, and later decline until death. Furthermore, we are immediately born again through a transformation – much like the passing of the seasons. In author Floyd Merrell's words, 'Spring gives way to summer, summer to fall and fall, to winter.' And then it begins again, in the same order.

Seasons of nine years

We live our lives in chapters. Each one of these seasons, like a brand-new day, includes a new beginning and a unique opportunity in the journey of your life. If you can turn the page, leaving behind regrets, a new season will receive you with open arms, new ideas, new friends, new places, new projects, new challenges, and new possibilities.

The first time I came across the interconnection of cycles and human development was while studying a Waldorf's early childhood education course to help me while homeschooling my daughter. Research has identified stages of growth and spiritual development in humans. According to my own observation, I favor the theory of the cycles of nine years for the soul and seven years for the body, at the end of which it is said that all of our cells are replaced.

The soul experiences a series of cycles throughout life, each lasting approximately nine years. The first cycle of the soul takes place during the first nine years of life through the age of nine, the second cycle begins at nine and continues till the age of eighteen, the third from eighteen through twenty-seven, and so on. The sequences, which begin every nine years throughout a person's life, are unique to each soul and may not precisely follow these ages. Each cycle marks a new time, a new awakening with new lessons to learn. At the end of each period, we usually have some meaningful experience, a fork in the road, or even better, a 'proceed with caution' signal warning that significant changes are ahead. At the end of a nine-year cycle, the conditions that kept you tied to the former cycle end as well, and new situations or challenges open up for your further spiritual development.

Become more aware of the qualities and distinctions of your particular age and those around you. Notice the power of the beginning of a new season and how its decisive moments and intersections in the path of growth move you in a new direction. Suddenly you find yourself filled with new ideas or inexplicable wishes, like wanting to move, change jobs, or maybe to rest. Above all, it is the desire to adjust your direction in life to live with more balance.

If we fail to notice the rhythms and seasons in our lives, we will likely encounter setbacks in our travels. For example, if you feel as though your projects are not going anywhere during this year, maybe it's time to take a break, reevaluate your situation, and create new plans. If you sow during wintertime, the fruits of your labor will perish before they sprout. On the other hand, if you notice that your present year is filled with activities and opportunities, and you fail to take advantage of them, you may miss the chance to harvest in the next season. We can calculate seasons, but not always predict the details. We can anticipate that there would be a pause in winter, but we can't predict exactly when the cold wind will arrive or end. Winters can arrive early, they can overlap with spring and also fall, but they always begin, and they always end. One thing is for sure: you will harvest in fall when you sow in springtime.

The early years

Children also live in stages, as Waldorf, the Gesell Institute, and Piaget have all identified. During the first years, children naturally live in a fantasy world. It is through the use of our imagination that we make our dreams come true. A well-trained imagination during the early years ensures that we continue to enjoy the skill as adults. The imagination is the tool we use to bring dreams from the invisible world of belief to the tangible world of physical reality. Imagination is the capacity to dream a vivid, full-color reality, almost believing it to be real.

Unfortunately, society values a sharp intellect and a challenging academic education over imagination, including the premature use of memory and reading skills. Untimely competition, and excessive use of TV and electronic games, eventually win over imagination, leaving little time for creativity. In the early years, children learn naturally by imitation. A perfect time to inspire their curiosity through the arts and music, allowing them free time to play through their natural imaginary games (without the excessive need for a TV, tablet, or more screen time). Parents can encourage the use of the imagination through the art of storytelling – instead of reading to them or showing illustrated books. They can also inspire values by telling stories and fables that complement other education. I particularly recommend that you find inspiration in the classic fairy tales and then include Aesop's Fables, which apply ethical principles in a fun and easy way. Valuable lessons are learned from these stories, not just from the decisions made by the characters, but also from the consequences those decisions have in their lives. The child's imagination is impaired by ideas fed through movies, that will later sell them prefabricated toys as merchandise.

The child's energy during this time should be directed towards developing a love for nature and filled with free play; that is, games that are neither organized nor directed by adults. Simply put: allow the child to play, to be spontaneous and full of improvisation, just as he naturally does and is.

Before turning nine, children have reached most of the conclusions they will keep during their lives. At this stage, they learn skills by imitation and example. The formal education given at school is not as strong as the silent lessons that people around the children convey through their actions and behavior – prejudices and good or bad models to follow – begin in these early years. A despicable look at someone of a different race, a little lie at a supermarket, verbal abuse, or contact with aggressive or extremely submissive people are enough to build imbalanced adults in the future; thus, repeating destructive family patterns. Actions speak louder than words in the task of child-rearing.

From nine years onwards

A great change for a child occurs at age nine when he leaves the dream world behind in exchange for reality. In Waldorf education, this stage is known as 'the fall' or a paradise lost – a fall from the dream world. While imitation and example are an essential part of the first stage of development, after nine, a trusted source of authority will be indispensable for a child's growth. The child will feel naturally inclined towards an authority figure that comes from respect, instead of fear. The word 'authority' here doesn't refer to an 'authoritarian force', but to someone who will inspire in the child a consciousness of morality, values, good habits, and inclinations – that will create a solid foundation to build his character later. At this stage, the child looks at the world through the eyes of his mentors. Real authority figures such as teachers, parents, grandparents, or all those representing moral and intellectual strength in the child's mind – including characters celebrated in history and biographies – will determine the child's future consciousness.

Beauty is also a source of inspiration for the child, both the beauty of nature itself as well as an appreciation of aspects like colors in art, a musical piece, flowers, and the order of things. We must allow children's inner beauty to flourish spontaneously during this stage by discovery and not by forcing or overwhelming them with endless information and facts. Indeed, children are the hope of the future.

Dreamers until eighteen

Adolescence is the time to be rebellious and strive to be independent. It is when the illusion of separation brings children towards a desperate search for their own identity and true love. Adolescents are intense and volatile, but also inexperienced and innocent with dreams filled with magic and fantasy. Anything seems possible to an adolescent, and as they reach for their goals, they also soon discover the bittersweet taste of disappointment – a time when the adolescent may feel a sense of despair. In reality, it is only the beginning of another vital season of independence. Adolescents throw themselves into a power struggle with their parents and teachers with endless arguments. These word games are their way of learning to become adults. They practice facing conflicts and testing their new identity by confronting their parents in a safe environment. These are their first battles for independence before they venture into the real world and are indispensable parts of their rehearsal of their future life.

In their teen years, searching for their own identity and a sense of justice becomes a perfect moment for parents to guide them towards their purpose. We can accomplish this by sharing about the lives of great heroes of humanity like Jesus, Gandhi, Martin Luther King Jr., or scientists with high ideals for the good of the planet. Parents can also promote lessons on the power of resilience during their children's adolescence by telling their own stories of struggles as teens themselves. Since children no longer have an image of their parents as heroes at this age, this sharing is also the best way to get a teenager's attention. Be prepared to be challenged, and don't take their questioning personally; they are testing the world through you.

Younger teens can be very trusting, and in their eagerness to find justice, they can become easy targets to false mentors. In our enthusiasm to make them independent, we can't assume they can make the right decisions – this is not a moment to leave them completely alone. Unsurprisingly, it is not entirely their fault; research has found youth to be immature in their capability to see the consequences of their actions.[31] Parents should not feel guilty about interrupting when their child is exposed to a bad influence or a dangerous situation.

There is a lot of talk about children's privacy, but complete privacy is a privilege that is earned with maturity. It is better to err by being too invasive than by staying ignorant of your teens' whereabouts. We must walk closer to the world of our kids in this stage more than ever; stay watchful and attentive to the people or messages they are exposed to, which translates into communication. In this day and age, corruption is within their reach as never before, mainly through the free use of virtual technology. Develop a trusting friendship with your teen; it takes effort, but we can win back their trust by being present. Share

---

[31] Raymond Corrado and Jeffrey Mathesius, 'Developmental Psycho-Neurological Research Trends and Their Importance for Reassessing Key Decision-making Assumptions for Children, Adolescents, and Young Adults in Juvenile/Youth and Adult Criminal Justice Systems, Bergen Journal of Criminal Law & Criminal Justice, 31 December 2014, https://doi.org/10.15845/bjclcj.v2i2.707.

small details of love that will show them you are there for them. A trusted spiritual mentor or family member who has a way with teens can serve as another outlet of communication beyond the parents to help the adolescents on their way.

The lost ones

Once teens turn eighteen, young men and women may find themselves lost. When they are separated from their parents' nest, they become like orphans and begin searching for a love that will replace it. The focus during this period is on the ego, and the young may appear selfish. The young can appear self-absorbed and too busy to give, but they do expect to receive.

The search for purpose and reason begins as the teen comes 'out of age' around twenty-one. Deceptions and frustrations become part of the process. People do not always react the way they expect, and events don't always go their way. There is the realization that they are not as powerful as they thought they were. Due to a pattern of instant gratification in the modern-day upbringing, many youngsters of this age live in constant disappointment since their life is no longer as predictable. We want to protect them from themselves, but their mistakes are necessary. If premature success is attained in the twenties, it is probably not going to be satisfying. Their souls have yet to learn at that point that their fulfillment does not depend on exterior circumstances.

The young have an unparalleled inner sense of justice, they have propelled many changes in the world with their innocent sense of *everything is possible* views, that many adults have forgotten.

The conquerors

Around twenty-seven, we make up our minds to follow a more defined direction as to where we want to go, though it may not always be aligned with our true mission. With all our strength, we charge forward just like Don Quixote against the windmills, conquering heroes while striving to attain our goals. This stage is easily identified by its constant action, work, and demonstration. We feel the need to be accepted. To prove ourselves to others, we try to appeal to the people around us through our pursuit of achievements and material possessions. This stage is centered on work, and we usually search for associates or allies to help us fulfill our goals.

The nest seekers

Close to thirty-six, we are getting near to reaching some stability. The fruits of our labor will give us some freedom to pursue the building of a home, a family, or the pursuit of a social cause. Now we have the maturity to leave our mark in society through our own identity. Career-wise, many will have found their place in society. The youth and energy of the mid-thirties are conducive to attaining our goals – evidenced by new generations waiting to get married later in life. The focus here is on family and community of friends with whom we share the fruits of our goals.

The explorers

Reaching forty-five is a well-known stepping stone for reaching spiritual awakening. As we get closer to our middle years, our fast world continues to slow down. Even if this slowing does not show up as a physical change, a stage of reflection will follow. A constant lack of satisfaction brings us to question the path we have chosen. At this point, we might see some abandoned successes. Some at this stage will turn from outward world success to inner search. We plunge into a journey of self-discovery where we ask ourselves if our lives have indeed been worth it and if our purpose has been accomplished. The focus at this time may turn outwards towards others. We ask ourselves, 'What can we do for our family and others?' and we begin anew.

This stage could turn into a real rollercoaster of changes, unstable achievements, and breakups. It is a new, however brief adolescence. This stage is known as the 'midlife crisis' for a good reason. We might renew our wardrobe, buy a newer model of car, or change our surroundings, convinced that this is our last chance to find ourselves and live again.

Our kids have probably left the nest at the end of this cycle, and our homes become uneasily quiet. The absence of distractions can reveal areas of our lives that were not working – showing us that life is brief and that our greatest riches are the small moments in time. We begin to realize that the real secret is to enjoy each present moment fully.

The sages

This cycle of wisdom begins at fifty-four, usually inspired by an important event. We begin to understand that we are not what we do or what we have, but the sum of our experiences and the result of what we have sown, who we have loved, what we have given, and what we have received. At the same time, we understand that we are the result of what we did not give and the chances we did not take. An acceptance process takes place during this stage, coming to terms with what we have indeed chosen to live with our virtues, limitations, and failures. Most of us reach a place where we desire to live life as who we indeed are, accepting the good and the bad without the need for false appearances or explaining ourselves to others. We finally let go of the life we did not choose and enjoy the life we have. At this time, we reflect and reach profound conclusions about the true meaning of life and what is truly important to us.

Our children already have lives of their own, and we no longer grieve over their departure. We now understand many of the reasons behind everything that was not, as well as everything that could have been. Now we have more time to do the 'trivial' things we always wanted to do – something that brought us joy but maybe not much material benefit. We enroll in a guitar course or the photography lessons we dropped. We write poems or stories, volunteer to help needy children, or perhaps decide to leave a legacy behind for a better world. It is a period of hiatus in the middle of your life, where accepting others as they are, comes more easily to us, without judgments or expectations.

Many indigenous cultures consider women after fifty-four to be wisdom keepers. If you have done your spiritual work and feel fulfilled, then you may become a wise one in this cycle. Intuition sharpens, particularly in women, as has been chronicled in many ancestral cultures. You begin to share your insights and life lessons with others, particularly the youth, often becoming their mentor by showing them how to achieve their hopes and dreams. Great legacies have come out of this cycle.

Love in this cycle is expressed by creating a haven for others at home; it is an oasis in time to enjoy life, travels, and peaceful activities, be it going solo, together, as a couple or in the company of the family. There are no complaints at this time since a new honeymoon begins, whether you are alone or in a love relationship. You now have time to enjoy your life, your sensuality, spirituality, and your present time – which is the only thing you truly have.

The alchemists

This cycle starts around sixty-three and marks the beginning of a magical time that reaches its peak after turning eighty when we return to our original home towards true fulfillment. If we become grateful for the present moment, this state of inner abundance is available at any point during our lives. After seventy-two, illnesses and passing of dear friends or acquaintances frequently remind us that nothing lasts forever, that everything ends and is transformed. You realize that the only thing you truly have is the now, the present time, and is also a time when we receive the fruits we have sown, either financial, physical, or emotional. We now become alchemists, transforming coal-like experiences into diamonds of learning. In this stage, we enjoy the beauty of music, conversation, painting, a flower … Time is all too important now and cannot be wasted on anything other than the enjoyment of your significant others company, grandchildren, and friends – together with sharing favorite hobbies, nature, concerts, service, laughs, and silence. This cycle is also a time to leave a personal legacy.

The magical years

Around eighty-one, those who have lived in spiritual consciousness and planted healthy seeds of harmony and love in their lives will reap and enjoy a new and more profound spiritual awakening. They will benefit from an eternal youth – some may even still be able to participate in some of their favorite activities even when the body doesn't cooperate. Joy is beyond the body. On the other hand, others beyond this stage will have to revisit infancy once again before returning to their origin. Some will experience being without memory or fundamental skills to survive on their own; therefore, requiring assistance to walk, eat, and take care of their most basic needs. This last experience on dependency is a final lesson for the person affected as well as for his or her relatives before ending a full physical life cycle.

A new rebirth

From a purely earthly perspective, death is the end of the last cycle. Most are afraid of death, avoiding even mentioning the word, unrealistically hoping to live forever. Our aversion to death has slowly morphed into denial. Western society teaches that someone's passing is a sinister and tragic event when it actually is the most significant and magical moment in a person's life. Death is undoubtedly a rebirth. Like a caterpillar, we shed our old shell and gain wings. If we had left behind our earthly attachments, it is a moment of celebration.

While it is true that we will miss a loved one, we need to be prepared for the fact that death in this world, is as certain as birth. All of us will eventually depart, and some will leave before others. We cannot control the time of death. The idea of keeping someone alive forever, or artificially when the person can no longer sustain themselves on their own, is not natural. Along the same line, we cannot kill or keep a body alive through our wills. Regardless of how death comes about (old age, a long illness, a sudden accident), I believe that death is a special event, both in the heavenly planes and here on Earth. Since Heaven is beyond time, beings of light can foresee death and are at work in that apparent succession of coincidences that happens when someone departs, guaranteeing that those left behind receive all the support and assistance they need to overcome their mourning. Sometimes, the passing occurs precisely a moment after a relative decides to leave the room. For example, many convalescing prefer to draw their last breath when their loved ones are not present. This event is not coincidental, angels and heavenly companions – usually the dying person's friends and relatives who have already left their physical bodies – are present at that moment of departure. They are aware of the pain and attachment their relatives have, which sometimes makes these events harder for all. Other times, however, the situation requires that relatives be present until the final moment.

It is not unusual to find that after the death of a relative, a newborn arrives. Other times the return of a long-lost member in the family will fill the void left, or even a new partner, a marriage, or a unique opportunity. Frequently, a loved one's passing coincides with the beginning of a new purpose, as when relatives of the departed one decide to pay homage to the deceased by leading a cause in their name.

After the surprising and tragic death of his best friend, writer Luis Miranda concluded: 'Sometimes, it is death that brings meaning to life.'

THE STORY OF WATER

People's lives are similar to a drop of water, which begins its journey as a transparent mist (spirit) with a longing to become like the flowing water; and hence it does, by way of condensation (it's birth). Once it becomes a drop, its adventurous journey begins through the soil, rocks, mountains, and the heavens (purification process). Much like human beings, water is transformed according to its experiences. Water can become part of a peaceful lake and, at other times, of a furious rainstorm. There are moments when the drop feels the coldness of the ice, and there are moments in which it explores the burning of the sun. The melting away under the unforgiving heat simply elevates the drop of water into the heavens to become the elusive mist it was when it all started.

A tear may experience hardness and heaviness in hail, yet it is also sheltered in the softness of the clouds and the salty healing of a teardrop. Some drops get to the ocean while others are left behind beneath the lower layers of the Earth. The same thing happens with humans. Some will face the seas with courage, while others will remain in the shadows, hidden inside the Earth, under the safety of its depth. Given the inevitable law of life's seasons, all water drops and all humans will inevitably transform themselves to finish their journey, and to return to their original form – the drop of water returns to mist, and the human body returns to spirit.

> *Birth and death are not two different states.*
> *They are two aspects of the same state.*
>
> — Mahatma Gandhi

If we could visualize the time of our death with our spirit eyes, we would see the truly magical moment – when the gates of Heaven are wide open, and everything turns to color and light. Some may even feel this magic while in the presence of someone else's passing. Ideally, we should make an effort to assure the dying person that all pending issues, debts, children, or any resentments, will be duly attended. Those who depart need to know that those who stay will be all right.

Sadly, hospitals many times do not have adequate space to respond to that special moment of utmost transcendence – a time when a human being has finalized his journey and graduated from all the seasons of life on Earth. Dear ones who have already passed return to guide the newly deceased, on the journey through the tunnel of light.

In some cultures, it is common to hear prayers, words of gratitude, and even celebrate death. There are two excellent gifts we can give our dear ones before they pass. One is to help them connect with God's light by way of prayer, either with the Lord's Prayer or the practice of your tradition – which will lead the soul to the light. The second gift we can give is to assure the passing soul, their surviving family will continue living with joy, and the certainty that they will meet again. Heaven is not a place that is too far, but an elevated state of consciousness beyond a veil – a new cycle begins in the spiral of life.

Life on Earth is brief, and we will reap only the spiritual fruits of the seeds we sowed. The soil and all physical tools we used to plant and gather our fruits will remain together with all the other things on Earth that don't belong to us. It is best to live a full life so we may die peacefully.

The seasons and our relationships

When we do not understand the cycles, especially in our partner's or children's lives, we may expect them to feel and react inconsistently with respect to their current lifecycle. Not knowing the dynamics of our partner's stages and seasons could create such a lack of understanding that it could end a relationship. Let's look at Isabel, thirty-three, and her forty-five-year-old boyfriend Carlos – a clear example of such a couple. Isabel is going through the period of pursuing her dreams, while Carlos has already lived through his stage of conquering, and might be arriving at his midlife crisis. He is currently feeling dissatisfied or, at least, questioning himself, wondering if the choices he made were worth it. He is on a quest for his mission in life and searching for meaning. Both motivations are just as valid in each of their particular stages. Conflict will arise if Carlos judges Isabel's conquering impulses as cold and self-centered or if Isabel questions Carlos's lack of decisiveness. To top it off, Isabel's mother, sixty, does not quite understand Isabel's many ambitions and is continuously urging her to live without much bother. Isabel feels caught in the middle of two different concepts of the world, which ends up draining her energy.

Once we know other people's seasons and understand that we don't swim at the same rhythm, we will be able to allow one another the freedom to travel the seasons in peace, at their own pace and without negative intervention.

Even when we intend to follow God's plan and observe the seasons, we may still encounter stormy and uncertain waters. The difference stems from no longer fighting against or being dragged by their currents since we know we can always invoke the Divine wisdom to guide us. Thus, we must invite and accept God's guidance in our lives at all times. God is above all seasons.

11

RULES OF THE GAME OF LIFE

ONCE UPON A TIME, THERE WAS A SOCCER PLAYER WHO HAD one big goal in his life; he wanted to be the best soccer player in the world. He trained to learn the latest techniques of the game and continuously practiced complex exercises. One fine day, the coach finally gave him the chance to play, and at the onset of the game, he scored an impressive goal. All he could hear was the loud roar of the spectators, and he smiled. The player closed his eyes to receive what he was sure was a standing ovation, until he was suddenly hit in the face with a tomato. As he looked around, he realized the audience was actually booing him. Bewildered, the player couldn't understand what was happening. He headed back to the team huddle, but the coach waved him over to the sidelines and pulled him out of the game.

'Coach, what are you doing?' asked the player, confused. 'I just scored that amazing goal!'

'It was amazing, all right,' replied the coach, visibly upset. 'The problem is you scored it for the wrong team!'

The player was so much absorbed in his technique and in his selfish need for attention that he forgot to pay attention to which team he was playing for and what his position was in the game. This story is an excellent example of how many of us live our lives. There are no favorable winds if you don't know where you are sailing. In the same way, even the latest or most sophisticated techniques for meditation, materialization, and alchemy will not serve you well if you don't know your team and the goal of the game.

As in life, to play the game, we must first know who we are and where we stand. Since we are all part of a team, to win the game, we must learn to work together to reach the same final goal. It will also be helpful if we understand the rules of the game. We need to be able to identify our position, our mission, and our purpose in this game of life. True, it will be wonderful to learn the laws that govern our universe, but it is more important to find out which team we belong to. There are two teams: God and us. We must ask if our actions are serving God and The All or living for the goals of the ego and ourselves.

The difference between dreams and desires

We all have the right to follow our dreams. Still, we need to ask ourselves the true intentions behind some of our dreams. Are they born from our inner selves, or are they *a want* from our ego? To know the difference, first, it is vital to connect to His Will or the *highest consciousness*. Dreams that are born from our soul proceed in a natural and effortless way.

There are two ways to manifest dreams in life: the *old way* – create things utilizing our own will – or the *new way* – allow God's perfect plan to reveal itself naturally. The seed of a tree does not create, plot, or manipulate. When we align with the Will of God, the main focus is to get out of the way to allow His guidance.

How can we align ourselves with His plan? One way to contentment is to be flexible and accepting of *what is*. When we surrender to the soul's plan, it automatically brings the favorable conditions we need to fulfill it. The new life's adjustments may not always be to your liking, but they will always bring real peace. For example, if you are working for a company that expects you to work extra hours, keeps you from spending time with your family, or makes you sell products against your moral or ethical values, you will probably choose to change jobs. If you decide to stay in the wrong position regardless of the contradictions, chances are you will lose the job without your intervention. Frequently an apparent loss is really an opportunity in disguise towards your true dream and purpose. A desire is different from a dream because it originates from attachment, which lacks wisdom and may not be in harmony with your true plan or that of others. A goal born out of attachment is always followed by pain and anxiety, whereas your highest expression will always bring joy because it is part of a perfect plan: God's plan.

> *A dream is born out of a full heart in order to give, whereas a desire comes from an empty heart, in order to receive.*

According to Dada, my teacher from India, the best way to build a dream instead of a desire, is to pray for direction: 'Protect me, dear God, even from my own dreams.' A dream's only purpose is to fulfill our true destiny by allowing the Will of God. While you learn to discern between dreams and desires, our goals should only be considered as an option, where you are detached from the results. When we grow attached to a specific outcome, the desire can end up consuming every part of your life – the formula for excessive ambition. Therefore, dreams should only be a preference, not a requisite for happiness. To be free from painful attachments, be sure that your dreams do not depend on anyone other than God. Often, we don't know where a dream comes from or its implications upon attaining it, only time will reveal the truth.

Here is an example: Richard dreams of becoming the president of the company he works for. Deep down, Richard feels he was never his dad's favorite son. He subconsciously believes that by becoming the president of the firm, he will prove himself of value to his dad (subconscious, egotistical belief). Richard never has time for spiritual growth. He has never consulted God or asked about His Will and His plans for him. Richard simply works tirelessly to reach his goals. He doesn't realize that to attain his desires, he does things that are inconsistent with his integrity – including taking clients out to dinner several times a week and completely neglecting his family.

One day, an important client invited him to a brothel. Unable to say no for fear of losing this client's business and consequently his boss's approval, Richard accepted. His wife found out, and understandably became very upset. After putting up with her husband's absence for the thousandth time, she finally decided to send him the divorce papers. Ironically, the very day he lost his family, Richard received a promotion to become the president of the company. Richard felt like the most miserable man on Earth with new offices overlooking the bay of New York. Even though he had reached his dream – or better said his most expensive desire – he felt like the biggest loser on Earth.

Richard had more chances of keeping his integrity if his consciousness was supported by God's wisdom. When we know that God is the source of all our good, we are not as attached to the result. His faith in God would have been stronger than his desire. Richard should have said: 'God, I have a preference. I would like to be the president, whenever you deem it appropriate and if it follows your plan, but not if I violate my own integrity.'

Who knows if the perfect person for the post was not Richard but a different president? Who knows if his desire prevented the company from having a better direction? The fact is that only God knows the outcome; thus, we should always consult with Him about all of our dreams.

The Law of Attraction – or is it the Law of Distraction?

This very popular law is based on the belief that every object has its vibration. The Law of Attraction shows how to induce a distinct vibration through the will by using a specific technique to alter our vibrations – to attract what we seek. How can we be certain that what we want to attract is genuinely the best for us? The problem with using our wills to attract dreams is that we can only wish for things, events, and people according to our present state of consciousness. If a drug dealer learned of this law, he would surely use it to make his business grow. He might very well reach his goal because laws work in an impersonal way. However, according to another law – the Law of Cause and Effect – there would be terrible consequences for all the kids who become addicts and also for the drug dealer himself. Likewise, if we show this Law of Attraction to a woman with low self-esteem and uses it to attract a mate, she will most likely attract the person least appropriate for her, someone she will desire regardless of the consequences. We naturally attract the persons and situations that mirror our inner state of mind.

There are two opposing ways of using the Law of Attraction. One is by using our limited power without God's help. The other is to allow our highest expression to manifest itself through our connection to God naturally. When choosing God's ways, His very intelligence will bring us the most favorable outcome every time.

In matters of reaching our dreams, God always has a better idea.

We can achieve better outcomes by allowing God's Will to surprise us with His infinite grace. When we force our will, we stumble upon what I now call the 'Law of Distraction', a technique that will inevitably lead us astray from our highest good.

But seek first His kingdom and His righteousness,
and all these things will be given to you.

— Matthew 6:33

The genie of the magic lamp

One day, I realized that I was using the universal mind as if it were a genie in a magic lamp. Instead of asking God, I was demanding all my wishes to be delivered at once. I realized that to find true happiness, I had to do the exact opposite, instead of expecting the genie to please me, I had to learn to look up to the heavens and say: 'My Lord, your wishes are my command. Your Will be done in me!'

Surely Dada, my spiritual teacher, knew the answer. Every time I asked him about the secret laws of the universe, he would smile. Pointing his index finger to the sky, and patiently saying: 'Sharon, God is the secret.' Now I understand that only God knows what is truly best for me. We are all connected and have access to a field of latent possibilities. But the ego can create problems as well as good experiences. The difference between manifesting positive or negative experiences come from your intention, and, like the story of the soccer player, you need to be clear which side you are on. Someone can be aligned with the Divine plan and become a spiritual leader like Gandhi, or make a pact with the dark forces and turn into a destructive one, like Hitler.

Power without consciousness is destruction. Values, love, and positive intention make the difference between a dream and a desire. Having a dream doesn't entail controlling or manipulating the will of other people. I am referring not only to the persuasive powers of some political and advertising campaigns but those who resort to witchcraft. Out of desperation, many people turn to black magic to achieve their dreams, dangerously placing themselves in the hands of self-proclaimed witches, wizards, and shamans, who sell potions and rituals. We all have a right to find ways to feel better, but we must beware of breaking spiritual laws. Any action attempting to influence or interfere with another person's individual choice or free will is not from God, because not even He interferes with the right to free will of any human being.

PART IV

THE CONNECTION PROCESS

12

SEVEN STEPS TO CONNECT WITH YOUR LIFE'S HIGHEST PURPOSE

WE ALL HAVE AN ORIGINAL IMAGE, AN IDEAL BLUEPRINT perfectly embedded within us. Contrary to popular belief, your highest expression is revealed, not created. Just like the seed of a tree, you have a perfect inner original design that is just waiting for the right conditions to express itself. We forget our original image when we adopt one that is foreign to our true Self.

The Connection Process: Seven Steps to Connect with Your Life's Purpose

I have found the seven-step sequence of the Connection Process to be a valuable path to a turning point in your life. I inadvertently discovered this sequence while helping friends identify their true purpose. Even after walking various spiritual paths, I had never encountered such effective, if not miraculous, steps to reach one's true purpose. Before this technique, I had tried many others, including the age-old visualization technique for manifesting, also known as the

Law of Attraction. Yet, I never felt completely satisfied with this method. Even when some of my dreams materialized, they did not result in lasting happiness – since it did not address the root of my dissatisfaction. Often it made the situation even worse. I felt like a clumsy alchemist, and the expression of 'Be careful what you ask for,' suited me well. Later I realized that my biggest mistake in the formula was omitting the most critical ingredient: God.

When I began letting go of my own limited guidance in favor of His Will, my life slowly began to move towards a more positive life experience. I must admit that at the beginning, the changes did not always appear to be positive. I had to learn to let go of many things that, in principle, I thought were good for me. Likewise, I learned that any process might be a challenge if we don't allow certain situations to leave our experience. Working on ourselves is about decluttering, making space for His power. In the process, I learned to let go of acquaintances, relationships, places, and situations that didn't suit me anymore. Now I realize, this is an ongoing process. You can't expect to live a new life while making the same foolish choices that got you in the adverse situation in the first place. With Him, all things are good. When walking with God, even amid the turmoil, be rest assured that all things will work out in your favor. Although the reasons behind the chaos are not always apparent, trust that further along the road, God will reveal the truth.

There is always room to grow. Even when you feel content with your current state of affairs, I assure you – there is always an opportunity for a higher expression of yourself. We must first ask for His wisdom to show us what needs to change – since we cannot change what we cannot see.

Understanding free will

Surrendering your will does not mean giving up your right to choose. It means inviting and granting permission for the higher wisdom of God to be revealed through you. The wisdom you are part of and also permeates the universe will show you the right choices through the power of love. I call this personal Higher Wisdom, God.

To live under this Divine guidance, we must first learn to surrender voluntarily to His Will. Only by granting our permission may God intercede in our lives. Even if we are about to jump off a tall building, God may warn us, but will not stop our wrong choices. That is the law: He granted us the power of free will, which allows us to make our own decisions at all times, even against our own good. What then is the purpose of free will?

> *Free will is the power God grants us so that by our own wills, we may return to His, again and again.*

When we learn to let go of our imaginary control, we realize there is a higher order at work in the universe. Humility is seeing that no matter how hard we try, we can't move the stars, advance the phases of the moon, or delay the arrival of each dawn. Whenever we are not connected, and in harmony with God's Will, our own unaligned decisions get in the way of the full expression of love that is available through us. Attempting to control the world is the opposite of allowing this natural order to manifest in our lives.

Letting go of this false need to control is the only logical solution since an unconnected free will only succeeds in blocking all the goodness that God has in store for us. A clear example of this is the current state of our planet. We are living on an Earth that has depleted its resources as a result of all the insanity and wrong choices we have made through greed. An ailing free will that is not guided by the wisdom of love will be ruled by ill beliefs and fears of the mind. What most people believe to be a manifestation of their free will is usually a reaction to fear – not a conscious decision guided by love.

The solution to this situation is to let go of the arrogance and illusion that we can manage this universe by ourselves without Divine help. Instead of carrying the world's weight on our shoulders, we can choose to work together through our collective free wills aligned to God's. More and more people must unite their wills of love together, accepting their role as a grand instrument for the good of all. Only His intelligence understands the position each of us must occupy in this world to advance together, unified as a planet.

When things are going smoothly in our lives, we rarely stop to think about the alternative of allowing God's Will. Only when things go wrong, we consider calling God in prayer – the moment when we raise our hands to the heavens and cry, 'I cannot do this anymore. I surrender all to you.' Ultimate surrender also coincides with the moment we see miracles happening. Surrendering your will to God does not mean abandoning your dreams or surrendering your right to choose. It only means that you freely choose to allow God to guide your every action. When you become a natural channel for His expression, it is a two-way invitation. God calls you inasmuch as you call Him.

At times people say to me, 'But I surrender my will to God all of the time, and nothing happens. God doesn't answer.' They often fail to see that by being worried; subconsciously, they are not surrendering all of their wills – since a strong attachment mixed with anxiety will interfere with this process.

Anxiety is the telltale sign of not surrendering.

The steps described in the next section will help you access this connection to God, time after time. Surrendering is not a one-time event. It is a lifetime commitment to your inner voice. When you surrender to God and His guidance, you immediately feel your burdens lift, and peace takes the place of your worries.

Follow these steps with faith and sincerity, begin by looking at a situation or emotion that keeps you from true peace at the present moment. All the previous chapters were a preparation for the practice of the following steps. Consistently connecting to the Will of God will lead you to a fulfilled life.

Connection Process Step 1: Self-observation

Stop for a moment and breathe deeply several times until you are relaxed. Keep still and observe the situation you have chosen without being reactive or judgmental.

Experience the emotions and notice in what part of your body you are feeling them. The first step to healing is the ability to feel your feelings. Continue the silence and begin to connect with God so that He may guide you. Ask Him to give you a new set of eyes and place your attention within. Do this objectively, without blame – make an effort to stay neutral while you examine the habits and behaviors that brought you to this specific situation.

Connection Process Step 2: Acceptance

Life may be lived at different levels of consciousness, the lowest being when you believe in having no control over what happens to you and consider yourself a victim of all your circumstances. In this state, you live from the perspective that only bad things happen to you and that it is all because of your bad luck. You either blame others or believe that God is punishing you. Acceptance is the highest level of consciousness. It is living from the perspective of true responsibility and light, knowing that many of your achievements and failures are the sum of all the decisions of your past. Being responsible is not the same as blaming yourself by saying you had total control of these choices. We don't have control over the world circumstances, but we can choose our perspective. It is about the capacity of being able to respond positively to the unexpected. Acceptance is coming to terms with your current state of being. Everything you resist intensifies in strength. As the popular saying goes: what you resist persists.

Acceptance and resignation are not one and the same.

Acceptance is being responsible and acting with a positive and proactive outlook by assuming your life lessons with dignity and responsibility while keeping your reactions under control. We accept ourselves by owning our flaws, shadows, fears, and weaknesses, making peace with all of them. Observe yourself with all honesty, and see yourself just as you are today. Look at your weight, your health, and your financial status from an honest and nonjudgmental perspective. If you lost your house or your partner left you, accept it. Let go of denial, one of the ego's best friends, and embrace *what is*. Acceptance is the ego's worst enemy. Humbly accept where you are in the path, without denial or guilt. If you are fully aware and accepting of where you are standing in your life, you will be closer to seeing the next steps needed to advance in the direction of your dreams. Acceptance is searching for peace; the opposite is resisting or fighting the lesson. *Accept even when you are not accepting*. There cannot be a change without acceptance.

Connection Process Step 3: Be grateful

Be grateful for the things you have: health, love, a partner, a family, a roof over you, a pet, oxygen, etc. Thank the universe itself. The more you give thanks, the more you receive from life. Be grateful for your gifts, presents, virtues, and defects. Giving thanks is a compliment to God and nature. It is a way of confirming that *you* are aware of your connection with The All. I am not saying to be grateful for hardship, still be thankful in advance for the good God will bring from each lesson received – since even a fall can be a blessing in disguise when God shows you how to use it for your good. Each lesson learned takes you one step closer to your dreams. Let God know that you are willing to receive His miracles by being grateful. Everything has a reason for being. Remember that even stars and galaxies have an order to follow. Sometimes only by experiencing darkness can we gain an understanding of light.

Darkness is only a reminder to turn our faces to the light.

THE STORY OF THE CASTAWAY

Once upon a time, a castaway who lost everything in a shipwreck managed to swim to a deserted island. Little by little, he built a hut from palms and wood for protection. Day after day, he waited for someone to rescue him, but no one did, and his desperation increased. One day when he returned from fishing, he saw smoke in the sky. Running to see what had happened, he found his hut, his only possession, burned to the ground – this was more than he could take. Angry at God, the man yelled, 'What else are you going to take from me? I have nothing left!' He fell to the ground, sobbing.

At that very moment, a loud roaring noise from the sky above him brought his tears to an end. He looked up to see a helicopter landing a short distance from him. 'You've come!' he shouted to his rescuers. 'But how did you find me?' The pilot smiled and pointed at the smoldering ashes of his hut. 'We saw the smoke from the fire.'

Even if we can't see it from the beginning, being thankful is knowing that, even though it may not be apparent, there is an order to each lesson, a reason for concealing a gift that will make sense at the end of the journey – one that might change your life for the better.

Connection Process Step 4: Calling upon the Will of God

God's Will, is also known as the Highest Expression. The name we choose to call Him is not essential; there is only one God. What matters is that we understand that God is love. Surrendering doesn't mean giving up our rights to choose to a manipulative, impulsive, and unforgiving being. In the West, the false belief that God will take away all our good is a mistaken view, and many people are afraid to surrender to God's Will.

Following His Will means aligning with the best conclusion and possible result in any area of our lives. It is to flow in tandem with the rivers of His guidance. It is receiving assistance and wisdom to choose the best path – since it is not unlikely at times that what appears to be the best course may prove to be the wrong one. Feelings can be deceiving.

This step is about consciously inviting and calling upon Divine assistance, allowing and accepting the solution through His inspiration. As we have seen, we all have free will, and even God won't intervene if not consciously invited. God always has the right answer. The secret lies in granting our permission. His assistance will be delayed if we do not freely allow Him to enter into our lives and take on our challenges.

The real reason many believe that God is silent to their prayers is they haven't learned the power to allow.

Everything in life is a possibility, a latent potential. Life is a blank canvas where you can draw the most beautiful masterpiece or create the darkest valley. Once you walk with God, you still hold the brush in your hand and the ideas in your mind. You are still painting each stroke, but if you allow God, He will give you the blueprint, show you the vision of the finished masterpiece and gently guide each stroke of your hand. Why doubt His energy and guidance, if He is the True Creator who painted the perfect masterpiece of the whole universe and the Curator who also designed the best picture of your own ideal life, much before you even imagined it?

Call upon the Will of God into your life and surrender the guidance of your own free will to Him. The distinction between asking for an outcome and simply allowing His intervention in your life will make a difference in the answers you receive. Give your permission with all your being as you pray the following prayer of connection earnestly, as you would in a solemn ritual. Pray it in a way that suits you best. Go to the synagogue, a temple, church, or a mosque. Or pray inside your home, with or without candles. It is the same, regardless. You can do this at any time or anywhere and as many times as you find necessary. Your personal religion and beliefs are irrelevant, as is the form in which you see God and the way you decide to call upon Him. This prayer will reach Him. There is only one God, and he will answer your effort.

THE CONNECTION PRAYER

My Father, I call upon Your Celestial Presence so that it may be present in my whole being at all times. I allow Your Will to be done in all areas of my life. At this moment and always, I allow all of your wisdom to work through me. I invite your Higher Will to guide, bless, and protect all of my personal relationships, my family, my finances, my purpose, my health, my physical surroundings, my service, and my spirituality. I surrender my mind, thoughts, emotions, and spirit to Your Wisdom, so that You may harmonize them in Your Light. I accept becoming an instrument of Your Plan through Your Will, expressing this way my highest potential through Your Presence within me. Use me in ways unimaginable to me. Make me an instrument of Your Plan; take my talents, hands, voice, eyes, ears, brain, legs, and imagination, and bless them with Your Highest Will of love. Amen!

You have surrendered your guidance over to God, and this is a magical moment, now you can laugh or cry with joy. It is essential to consciously surrender the seven areas in your life: your body and health, your abundance, spirituality, your service, your personal relationships, your family, and your true purpose. Do it with faith, and after you have surrendered, completely detach from the outcome. Your intention is the most critical part of the process. When you say I SURRENDER, you are granting your permission and aligning your free will to His, and that is the distinct component that works a miracle.

If you feel that you are not ready to surrender all areas of your life, if you feel any sort of resistance, modify this prayer and use the words I AM WILLING instead of I

SURRENDER. That is all God needs to hear, to enter into your life. A tiny spark is enough to light up a dark room. The connection is always there, but we separate ourselves from our good whenever we doubt, are afraid, or wish something against our plan. Because of this disconnection, we need to be alert and willing to reconnect and surrender as many times as is necessary, especially if we feel anxiety during the day, an accurate indicator that we have strayed away from guidance. When we try to fuel our energy from things and goals that are not aligned with our highest good, we feel depleted. When our source of energy comes from desires instead of our vision, it will feel like we are connected to a weak battery instead of God's mighty power, which never runs out. Surrendering to God provides an eternal source of energy, peace, and true immunity against all attachments.

Once you allow God to work in your life, expect inspiration, ideas, new outlooks, and people with a message. Choose now to act responsibly to fulfill your mission. Allow yourself to be led. You may begin testing your new choices with small daily acts, choosing with the firm will that you have now received. It doesn't mean that you will be exempt from mistakes, but not being attached to an outcome will minimize your errors.

Connection Process Step 5: Forgiveness

Forgive yourself for the situation you are at the moment. No one is perfect; none of us are. We are here to learn and let go of the shadows that temporarily diminish our light. Today, make a choice to forgive all of those involved in the situation that you would like to heal.

When we forgive ourselves, we love ourselves. When we forgive others, we free ourselves and others. We don't have real power to bestow God's absolution upon another human being. God doesn't use condemnation or punishment. He forgives those who wish to be forgiven because when we ask for forgiveness, the mere acceptance releases us from our pain. God does not blame, just as we don't blame a small child for his errors. Of course, ignorance of the law will not save us from some consequences. From God's point of view, forgiveness is not a privilege granted, but a lesson learned. A lesson in forgiveness may take an instant or an eternity. 'I will see you in Paradise,' Jesus said to the criminal on the cross. The process of realizing your own mistakes is a personal affair with God. We also don't know for certain what has led the other person to do the unforgivable, which in no way justifies the wrong action.

> *If we knew how to understand, it would not be necessary to forgive.*
>
> — Father Ignacio Larrañaga

We must understand that most of us fall victim to other once victims who, at some point, were similarly attacked; thus, creating a great chain of pain. Only God knows. Although God forgives, it is sometimes impossible to eliminate the consequences of a mistake. It does not mean that we won't denounce a crime – forgiving is not excusing others' behavior or exposing yourself to danger.

What we can do, however, is take responsibility for what we feel and be open to the possibility of letting go of the constant reminder that feeds our pain.

Forgiveness is not letting go of the offense; it is letting go of the hurt. Some offenses seem unforgivable at first glance – we can only forgive with the assistance of God's Divine grace.

Only God working through us can grant real forgiveness.

The true meaning of forgiveness

Forgiving is not the same as forgetting; it is letting go of the pain caused by the memory of the offense. It is normal to feel sadness, yet if you feel anger, blame, or reproach, you are still reliving the scene in your mind. Even though you may not consciously remember the hurt, it remains inside of you, quietly affecting your other relationships. You will recognize the moment you have forgiven the day you can tell the story as an anecdote and not as a tragedy.

Sometimes not the act, but the interpretation of the offense and the constant replaying of the thought in your mind hurts more than the actual act ever did. Someone might have hurt you, yet ultimately, no one outside of yourself can control your actions, reactions, interpretations, and challenges. Let go of the belief that you are a victim. You cannot control what others do to you, yet you can always choose a different perspective of the event.

The power we give to the attacker's actions after the fact is an interpretation, and frequently the real cause of the pain. If you were walking down the street and a drunk started yelling horrible things at you, you would probably laugh and pay no attention to him. However, if a person close to you does the same, you would probably feel offended and hurt, maybe throughout a whole lifetime!

Yet, as you can see, the act is the same. Only, in the latter case, you are giving others permission to hurt you through your own interpretations or the value given to the insult, allowing it to hurt you indefinitely.

Your attacker commits the mistake the first time. From then on, your lack of forgiveness makes you hurt yourself endlessly each time you remember.

When you don't forgive, you are chained to the person you despise, carrying them with you. Forgiveness is the only way to let them free. You are tied to this person with an invisible chord, and every time you remember, you send them your poison, but not without first poisoning your own body.

PRISONER OR GUARD?

Once upon a time, there was an island where only two people lived: one was an accused criminal, and the other was a police guard. The guard decided he had to put the criminal into a jail cell and kept him locked up. Since there was no one else living on the island, the guard had to stay day and night guarding the prison cell to make sure the criminal didn't escape. He began to realize this was a problem. Although he was a free man who had committed no crimes, he could not enjoy his freedom any more than the criminal. He had put himself in jail as well!

This same thing happens when we don't forgive: we not only incarcerate the other person, but we also imprison ourselves.

PRACTICE: STEPS TO FORGIVENESS

The only way to truly manifest the miracle of forgiveness is through God. Through His strength, we heal the pain of what another has done to us.

Maybe your pain is so intense that you think you are unable to forgive or are NOT willing to let go of the pain. You might consider making an effort to heal, knowing that you are harming yourself and possibly others. Lack of forgiveness over a particular situation is the leading cause of deadly illnesses – many have entirely recovered after a forgiveness process.

Open yourself to forgiveness: It is possible to forgive, even during times when you feel unable because all God needs is an opening in your heart. It is not about denying your feelings. It is about accepting them and being *willing*. Even if you feel incapable of forgiving an offense, three magical words will be enough to begin the process: *I am willing*. 'I am willing to forgive and to heal.' Start declaring these words and let go. Every time thoughts of the pain come back, repeat: 'I am willing to forgive through God in me.' Upon giving your pain to God, you will notice that at some point, He will provide you with the perfect opportunity to let it go.

***Feel your emotions, write them down, and burn them*:** Write down all of your experience on paper to complement the first step. Write as you feel each raging emotion without repressing it. For example: 'I am feeling a lot of pain; my chest hurts, my tears are salty. I want to scream!' You mustn't repress the pain. If you can feel it, you can transcend it; but if you suppress it, you will only keep it inside your body. Empty all of your rages, all of your frustration, and all of your thoughts onto that paper. Once you are done, burn the paper. Remember, this letter is not intended to be given to the person that offended you. As you throw away the ashes, state the following words: 'This too shall pass. I release and let go of all resentment.' Afterward, try to get it out of your mind; don't think about it anymore.

Pray for your enemy's wellness: Praying for the good of your enemy may seem to be the hardest thing to do. Regardless, make an effort, and when the person's image comes to mind, send love and pray: 'May God protect you, and you may find your highest destiny in love and happiness. That is my wish.' Perhaps your words won't immediately flow with sincerity, but rest assured that miracles will happen as you continue with the exercise. Many people hurt others precisely because they lack joy in their own lives. When these people find their happiness, they free those they hurt. Notice that when you send a love prayer to another, you first experience the love yourself. Love heals both of you. If you practice this exercise with faith, if you send love out, it is possible that the next time you encounter that individual, you will see a new person resulting from the real forgiveness you granted. Remember, you cannot control others' thoughts, choices, or feelings. You can only choose to see things under the prism of love.

Every so often, take stock of your life and ask yourself if there is resentment in your heart against another person, group, or entity. The goal is to have a clean heart, free of blame and resentment.

After you practice this technique, a truth about the situation you need to forgive may be revealed. It may arrive through an encounter or by receiving information from the past that may help you understand the situation better. Be alert, as this can happen at any time or place. If you find yourself with an opportunity to forgive and a moment of understanding about the situation arrives (forgiveness), you must be open and willing to accept the verbal or internal apology without fear or pride. Feelings of righteousness or anger may ruin the opportunity to release the parties from hate. Likewise, it is wise to wait for the right moment. Never pat an angry dog, for it will surely bite your hand. Simply pray, let go and wait for the right moment. If you rush forgiveness, you might encounter a wall; in the same way, if you wait too long, you may miss the window of opportunity. Waiting too long might prove to be too late, and resentment may just grow stronger. Under God's tutelage, there is perfect timing. Sometimes we are the ones who will be guided to take the first step in approaching the person who committed the offense. I have asked for forgiveness in cases that weren't entirely my fault, and the liberation was the same. If you feel a strong impulse to act, then pray and repeat beforehand: 'I am willing to let go of the fear of humiliation or hurt in exchange for my freedom regarding this situation.' I assure you that the exchange will be highly compensated. A hurt ego resulting from rejection is nothing compared to the constant pain of suffering.

Some meetings may not be advisable or in your best interest; for example, when you are involved with a criminal or someone who mistreats you. It is not recommended to meet an addict or someone who manipulates you or has some sort of unhealthy control over you. In cases of codependency or obsession, you should keep your distance from them and, if necessary, use the intervention of a professional.

You can even forgive a person who is not present, someone who is not conscious, awake, or responsive, a person in recovery, or even someone who already passed away since the soul never dies. We are all one, connected by invisible lines of the same network; these beings will receive all of your feelings, the good and the bad ones. Likewise, you will receive all corresponding replies to your feelings, affecting you the same way even when not aware of it.

I will never stop telling everyone about the incredible sense of well-being we feel each time we choose to forgive. In fact, the mere act of forgiving opens doors formerly closed to me and solved long-standing problems. I have also seen how the simple act of reading this technique has helped many to solve deep-seated, long-standing problems miraculously.

Connection Process Step 6: Letting go

This process is accomplished by totally surrendering the situation to God without any expectations, including the solution you are expecting or a specific reaction from the people involved. Detach yourself completely from the outcome. If you trust and can remove yourself from the situation – the fear, guilt, anger, and excessive self-compassion – it will all be resolved by God's intelligence, which is the same power that organizes the planets and the universe. Becoming detached from the result is not a way of inaction, resignation, or martyrdom; on the contrary, it is getting ourselves out of the way of miracles.

I am not saying that by letting go, you will allow God to handle everything and wait until he acts for you. We must make our own choices and actions, but they can be made through His guidance. While we walk in God's direction, we must also be open to making mistakes and learning from them, since it is only through practice, trial and error that we truly learn to discern and identify His right guidance.

THE STORY OF THE WISE MAN AND THE TRAVELER

While traveling through a desert, a man encountered a wise elder and began to ask him questions about God. He wanted to know about God's Will and whether we could trust in Him completely. The traveler asked, 'What should I do here in the desert while I sleep in my tent tonight? Do I let my camel loose or trust in God?' The wise man replied, 'Tie your camel and trust in God.'

Manage your belongings and whatever is important to you daily, walk in integrity, and be true to your values. Surrender your life to God, but live here and now, aware and dutiful.

Surrender your life to God, knowing that you have no control over how things will end. You can only control your attitude, where you place your attention and choices. Don't manipulate or try to solve things with your mind.

Let it all flow and allow the natural development of events. One thing, though: stay alert. Listen to your inner voice and act at the right moment when the signs are clear.

> *Surrender means, by definition, giving up attachment to results. When we surrender to God, we let go of our attachment to how things happen on the outside and we become more concerned with what happens on the inside.*
>
> — Marianne Williamson, *A Return to Love*

Reconnecting

Connecting to God is not a one-time process. If you feel your connection to God has been interrupted, you may reconnect anytime by repeating the Connection Prayer (see Step 4 of the Connection Process), or the ultimate prayer of connecting to God's Will: 'The Lord's Prayer'. If you are a Christian, you have probably prayed the words a thousand times, however just repeating some words automatically without knowing their intention will only keep them at the level of your mind, without rising to your spirit. When you pray from your heart, you feel the meaning of each word.

Reciting this prayer taught by Jesus, with the meaning and intention it was created for, changes your life dramatically no matter what religion you follow. Within the words, the prayer harbors all the necessary elements needed to be aligned to His presence. This prayer is the biggest secret! It invites the Will of God and immediately reconnects our purpose to God's essence.

The Secret Meaning of the Lord's Prayer

Our Father
Our only God. Abba, my Father, You are above all.

Who are in Heaven
You are at the highest level of the consciousness of love, beyond space and time. Omniscient and omnipresent.

Hallowed be Your name
Your name is sacred. You are the Holy of holies. I show You my reverence.

Your kingdom come
I call upon Your highest awareness, here and now. Your kingdom is inside of me.

Your will be done in me
I surrender my will to You, and I allow You to work in my life [the connection].

On Earth as it is in Heaven
May Your will be done and manifested in all areas of my life, as it has manifested in Heaven, where everything is perfect.

Give me this day my daily bread
I trust and depend only on You to meet all of my needs. I will not be anxious.

And forgive our debts, as we have also forgiven our debtors
Forgive me, Lord, as I forgive myself and others. Pour Your Divine Grace, and heal my trespasses.

And lead me away from temptation
Don't let me fall into doubts [disconnect] and follow the wrong dreams.

And deliver me from evil.
Keep me free from my ego, from division, from evil, hate, and fear.

Amen
Thank You, for You always hear me. So be it.*

---

* The Lord's Prayer, paraphrased. Matthew 6:9

Finally, be thankful again for having your whole life resolved in God's Will.

Connection Process Step 7: Spread the message

Imagine for a moment that God and His angels are looking down from the perspective of the heavens. Now imagine everyone on Earth is broadcasting rays of color according to the state of their souls. Let's say rays of red light and rays of green light are emanating from people. The color is like a call that identifies the state of consciousness. Those willing to be His instrument of unconditional expression will be sending green lights to Heaven, while those closed out from Divine energy and controlled by their ego will emanate dark red. What color would your ray be? Who will God choose as an instrument of love on Earth?

Once you connect to the Will, your life will change, regardless of what you feel you lost, be it health, a relationship, a dear one, your business or property. Gradually, you will see how your health will improve, finances will stabilize, and all areas will get back to their duly harmonious flow. You will once again have inner peace, which, in essence, is the most valuable treasure you can possess.

If you have everything but do not have inner peace, you have nothing. Yet if you don't have anything but still have God and His peace, you will have absolutely everything. Inner peace is the natural outcome of allowing the Will of God. Once in this state, all your true needs will be taken care of, and in the same manner, what hinders your evolution will automatically vanish.

The last step that helps you keep a lasting state of inner peace and connection is sharing and helping others find their connection. This cannot be done by preaching or proselytizing, but through the natural expression of your new Self. Spreading the word through your peace, your light, and your new values will spontaneously help others find their way.

When others notice something special about you that they like, you know you are emanating peace, the perfect time to share, by giving all recognition for your gifts, advantages, and success to the real source: God. This way, you are applying the virtue of gratitude and, at the same time, acknowledging the one who truly deserves all merits: God, the original source of all our blessings, the real meaning of humility.

THE REAL INVENTOR OF THE TELEGRAPH

In an interview, Samuel Morse, co-creator of the telegraph and signal coding bearing his name, was asked if he felt frustrated, lost, or at a dead-end during his university experiments. Morse replied with a solid 'Yes.' When asked what solution he found for those moments, he replied, 'I asked for some light.' He was then asked if God had helped him. He said, 'Of course He did. It is why I don't feel deserving of all the honors you grant me. God wanted to give this gift to humanity, and I feel grateful that he chose me to give it to the world.'

This interview helps explain why the first message Morse sent over the telegraph was: 'WHAT HATH GOD WROUGHT!'

God is searching for ways to bring millions of gifts to humanity in similar ways, through the hands of those willing to become His instrument. Morse simply had his 'rays of green light' towards Heaven ON, so God could see that Morse was granting permission to be used as an instrument, and he was chosen among many good scientists to imagine and bring this invention to fruition. Most important is the fact that Morse never forgot to give due credit to his source of inspiration. Imagination is the ability to recreate God's ideas here on Earth.

Each person you help along the way, plus those they support in turn, will bring more and more blessings. Blessings work like a magical, multilevel company. Whatever you do for someone today will be returned with the same intensity to you and others. The final goal is to create a chain of love that can light thousands of 'green lights' on Earth.

Living your daily connection with God

Living in this daily connection with God takes determination and practice. Even though most religions highly promote this lifestyle of allowing, very few people actually live in such total surrender. For example, some find it very easy to surrender their children's safety to God but cannot detach themselves from controlling their material goods. Others may easily surrender their health, yet cannot surrender their loving relationship to God, perhaps because they mistakenly fear that God will take their loved one away.

Paradoxically, when you are willing to consciously walk this path, offering all your burdens to God is the beginning of the simplest, most efficient solution to solving all of your problems, whether physical or spiritual: no exceptions.

By living this connection, many situations will be revealed for your highest good. Be willing to let go of what you no longer need. Just as in wintertime, leaves will fall from the trees – if you allow it, the people and situations that are not part of your highest path will leave you as well. Release them and let them go without pain, which is resistance. You can only suffer if you hold on and keep an attachment to something that no longer works.

Only God knows what relationships, jobs, or situations you should genuinely keep and which you must let go to allow space for something better to come into your life. It takes a lot of self-awareness and persistence to work from that perspective, yet the rewards are always better than the apparent loss. The road to living in connection with God may be easy or difficult, depending on how long you have been rooted in distorted desires or how much you have mentally invested in the wrong path of your old thoughts. You must now be willing to practice patience since the more you practice surrendering your will to God, the more your communications channels with Him will clear up. Living a miraculous life should be your natural state.

I have personally seen miracles happen since practicing this path of total surrender to God. By accepting His guidance unconditionally, I have seen how an impossible negative situation resolves with practically no intervention on my part. Everything I now need comes naturally, and the right information is revealed to me at precisely the right time. The answer always arrives when I ask with sincerity and also when I am willing to hear the real answer. His guidance protects me with an unexpected turn of events, even when I am about to make a terrible mistake and also after I err.

Trust and let go

Imagine a pilot who is used to flying an old manual airplane with its own set of operating tools. If allowed to own and fly a new automated jet, how would the pilot adapt to a new navigation method? It would certainly be a challenge for him to stop controlling his aircraft the old way and allow for a new, computerized system to take over the controls. He would feel uncertain during the first few days of flying this new automated plane, questioning himself and even interfering in the new control system manually. He would probably also want to go back to the old routine during those first few days, even though he knows that his old tools could never compete with the modern ones. The old plane had only one advantage; even though it was not as safe, it was very familiar. Once the pilot allowed the new intelligent system to guide him, he would have full view and access to a safe landing and even be able to fly and see through the thickest fog.

In the same way, people will eventually get used to surrendering control over their lives to God's wise hands. In the beginning, they will likely want to return to the old ways, especially during the first few months, but as time goes on, they will gradually begin to trust God's new traveling plan.

Changing the old lifestyle of being guided by the mind, the ego, and the emotions (the old tools) and beginning new guidance through our inner senses connected to God may have its challenges. Naturally, you will feel strange at the beginning. As you learn to adjust, your trust in God will grow inasmuch as you realize that the connection to

Divinity, as opposed to your confusing limited perception, is truly reliable, efficient, and infallible.

Remember, if you feel doubtful, lost, or disconnected at any time, repeat the words: 'I am willing,' with faith. That will suffice to reconnect with God.

TWELVE TOOLS FOR LIFE

THE REAL WORK BEGINS AFTER THE FIRST TIME WE MAKE a genuine connection with God. We are much like trees in need of light, nutrients, water, and protection to reach the sky. As humans, we have the same calling to reach His heights and highest expression. Like a growing tree, we also need to protect ourselves from unwanted weeds, like fear, rage, blame, guilt, worry, doubt, and stress. For this reason, you must acquire tools for strength and power that will help you eliminate any obstacles in your life.

In one of his books, Paulo Coelho describes us as light warriors, because indeed, that is what we are. We must face many battles to protect our peace and our lasting connection to God in the school called life. Every warrior has his weapons. The weapons of our enemy (the ego) are powerful and will be used to try to deceive us with a fear that is based on deceit, separation, death, and illusion. Yet, we have a powerful shield against them: our connection with God. These are the twelve tools that will serve you well in life:

1) Courage

Accomplishing your purpose is no small task. It requires a will of steel and the courage to *accept yourself as you are*, letting go of your past, and breaking free from your comfort zone. We all need the courage to live the life we were born to live, yet some of us develop fears through past experiences that can challenge us. It is essential to realize that these fears are not real, and once you identify them, they can no longer have control over you.

Our fears and their antidote

We carry unnecessary burdens, recurring thoughts and fears that we harbor, sometimes without our knowledge. If we become aware of our fears, we can change them. The more peace we have, the more healing we will experience. Each of our fears has a corresponding mistaken negative belief; in the descriptions below, there is also a positive statement, an affirmation that you can use to help harmonize it. Use your journal to identify your fears and write down the corresponding declaration next to each one. Most of us have more than one fear, and some are more prominent than others. The exercise is meant for you to *know yourself*.

Fear of losing physical security

Symptoms: This fear can present itself as fears of scarcity, of losing everything, and not being able to sustain yourself. It may even show up as acceptance of abuse for fear of losing security or placing financial benefit over love, health, and integrity, and even overwork. It can also show as obsessions and attachments about your home and properties. These fears create low self-esteem, insecurity, lack of self-confidence, selfishness, excessive frugality, excessive ambition, or greed.

Affirmation: I am enough. There is enough. I live in complete security because God is my complete source of abundance. He gives me my daily bread. He is the source of my peace, salary, income, and physical, emotional, and spiritual needs. I have nothing to fear. I thank God and freely share my blessings with others. I give God my fears about my livelihood. I am immensely grateful for all that I have, whether big or small, knowing that I will always have enough with Him.

Fear of losing emotional security

Symptoms: This fear may present itself with symptoms of addiction, eating disorders, need for sugar, alcohol, sexual dysfunctions or total lack of desire, emotional, unhealthy attachments; lack of creativity, guilt, inability to express feelings, jealousy, or feelings of loneliness; feeling insecure or having a wrong self-image – for example, feeling ugly or feeling overweight; obsession with the body, seeking pleasure; excessive exercise or plastic surgery.

Affirmation: I can express and feel my emotions in healthy ways. I accept myself, and I do not judge myself or others. I surrender to God all my personal relationships and fears of suffering or being rejected. Because God is my emotional sustenance, I am free from bonds and attachments. I take care of my body because it is a temple, but I don't allow it to be my owner. I freely express my creativity in a way that blesses others. I am free of the approval of others to feel my value. I am beautiful and have a healthy sexual image.

Fear of losing control

Symptoms: Fear of losing control may show up as anger, anguish, and anxiety, pessimism, lack of patience, fear of being controlled or desire to control others, or problems with authority, abuse, etc. It can present itself as fear of not being able to control others and contrarily, also fear of others wanting to control them. Some people with this fear don't have healthy limits for themselves; some may not respect others' boundaries. Also, they can have a lack of forgiveness, intransigence, and lack of will power, either in their inability to choose for themselves or a desire to choose for others. In other words, a lack of trust in God.

Affirmation: I allow God to take control of my life and my situation. Today I responsibly take control of my own life; I have confidence in myself, others, and God. My free will is guided by God. I choose and also allow others to choose. I do not need to manipulate or be manipulated. I forgive and let go. I trust.

Fear of losing love

Symptoms: Fears can appear as an imbalance in our ability to love, receive love, or nurture ourselves. Fear of loneliness can be revealed through jealousy, impulsive buying, or overcompensating for the love of others, problems in emotional relationships, codependence. It may also show us as a feeling of inferiority, anger, family attachments, lack of forgiveness, issues with employees or dependents, lack of self-love, etc. Lack of knowing how to set limits on emotional relationships or by showing doubt in God's love.

Affirmation: I love you. I love myself because I feel the love of God in me; therefore, I can love my neighbor healthily and freely without manipulating. My heart is clean, and God dwells in me; therefore, I can love and be loved without fear. God is my eternal source of love.

Fear of losing approval

Symptoms: The problems with this fear may arise due to lack of communication, the ability to express what you feel and your convictions, as well as because of insecurities about your skills. Also, not knowing how to listen, misunderstanding, fear of talking, or maybe talking too much. The uncertainty of taking a position, living in the mystery. It can show a lack of sincerity, or excess of it. Squandering, trying to buy opinion and acceptance.

Affirmation: I can communicate and fully express what I feel, speak confidently, and tell the truth at all times. I don't have to hide who I am or change to get approval from others. God approves of me; He speaks through my voice. My word is gold; I keep my word. I have full confidence in myself and others. I can ask and express my needs without hurting and without fear of being rejected. I can listen to others in silence and understand them. I can say no. I understand, and others understand me.

Fear of the future

Symptoms: This fear is due to a lack of spiritual vision, to be able to see and trust in what God has in store for your future. It also affects the imagination and causes problems like mental blurring, bad memory, and unclear vision. It may also result in resisting the past or the present, having anxiety about the future, not wanting to see a situation, fear of being paralyzed, not wanting to face reality, being in denial, as well as problems in discerning a situation.

Affirmation: I trust God to show me a beautiful vision of my future, a healthy conclusion of the past, and a clear view of the present. With His eyes, I see beyond appearances; I do not judge, but I can see clearly. I see myself as a being of light working on the purpose that I have to accomplish on this Earth. I serve others with love.

Fear of death

Symptoms: May occur due to lack of connection with God, inability to receive His direction, lack of spiritual connection, lack of faith, problems with your religion, lack of spiritual direction. Feeling of being away from God or not being in communion with His guidance and lack of faith.

Affirmation: I trust God fully. I live in communion with my God. I have faith. I have energy and vitality. I accept Your eternal guidance. I invite You to harmonize my life in Your Will, to remind me that I am a soul and that I live forever. I ask You to show me how to return to You; I believe in eternal life. I live fully without fear.

Not all symptoms are necessarily caused by fear. There is a possibility of other factors such as lack of proper nutrition, sleep, or sun, chemical or emotional imbalances, or a stressful event that may need to be treated by a professional. If there is any doubt, continue praying, but at the same time, you should seek help, which is part of loving ourselves and living in God's Will. His assistance arrives through the aid of others.

2) Your Thoughts

Thoughts are one of your most powerful tools. When thoughts are aligned and focused on goodness, they behave like rays of light, creating positive situations. Thoughts are not only voices inside your head but also a time machine, for everything you hold in your mind, whether peace or anguish, can very well turn into your reality in the future. Remember that even when thoughts are powerful, nothing is more powerful than allowing the Will of God.

3) Imagination

Imagination is the ability to be able to visualize clearly the plan God has for you. It is a gift we have lost and must urgently reclaim, to free ourselves from prefabricated images imposed by society and marketing interests. Imagination is also the blueprint for creating reality. When violence is encouraged in the imagination instead of peace, feeding it with harmful information, like violent video games, bloody movies, conspiracy theories, and books – an excellent tool will go astray.

Imagination is a vital ingredient, as it works as a virtual rehearsal in the creation of a new life, a new world, a new path, and a new way to solve challenges. Your voluntary connection to God will bring a keen vision to implement the most brilliant ideas. An enlightened imagination is continually sprouting new inventions to help the world – writing new stories to inspire goodness in others. An imagination that works together with the vision of God is enlightened. In contrast, an imagination without His vision is an empty vessel, searching only to be filled for its own benefit.

PRACTICE: HOW TO VISUALIZE

You may begin to consciously practice these steps once your connection to God is established since an imagination that is not aligned to God could be used inadvertently for the wrong end. The following visualization technique that uses imagination as a tool will help you in gaining access to God's vision for a better future for all.

Most people use the technique of visualization without realizing it. With his inner vision, a champion swimmer has seen himself standing on the podium a thousand times. Before receiving his medal, he mentally swam in the pool and saw himself lap by lap before physically doing so. An architect has seen a building in his mind, brick by brick, long before constructing it. You can visualize your purpose in just the same way. Relax in a quiet location and calm yourself with your breathing. You can do this anytime, though right before bedtime is advisable.

1. Ask God to confirm if your vision is in line with your purpose and His plan.
2. Center yourself inside your inner eye, as the observer.

3. Daydream and mentally practice the object of your visualization as you detach yourself from attaining it and leave it all to God.
4. As in the example of the swimmer, get under your skin, see yourself swimming, feeling the water on your skin, smelling the chlorine in the water, and tasting the water. Then see yourself at the podium, feeling the excitement of having attained your goal. Use your five senses and the resulting emotion. Replace the swimmer's vision with your own.
5. Thank God for what you have visualized and wait patiently to receive what steps to take to attain His goal.

I use this technique before speaking. Use it to create a strategy, a plan, or a legacy to help the world. But beware this is not the Law of Attraction. This technique is used subconsciously by many, even from physicians who visualize a complicated surgery. With the wrong mind, robbers could use this technique to rob a bank! It is imperative to be connected to God before getting the vision since the ego loves to deceive us with false dreams. Egotistical dreams never have a good outcome. Florence Scovel Shinn describes this perfectly in *The Game of Life and How to Play It*, with the example of a woman who desperately wished to live in her neighbor's house. She always visualized herself living there, and finally, she did: when her own house burned down, she ended up living at her neighbor's – as a temporary guest! So, don't ask for specific things unless there is a protection clause attached.

PROTECTION CLAUSE FOR A DREAM

Dear Father, I have a dream ...
If this dream is Your Will,
If it is part of Your plan for me,
I ask for this dream or a different one,
One you find more appropriate,
'Your equivalent' for me.
May this dream be in harmony
With everyone in it.
Protect me, God, even from
My egotistical dreams.
I accept the final outcome completely,
And I agree to let go of any attachment to it.
Thank You for listening, since
You know my dreams before I do.
Thank You for granting me the wish
Through Your highest Will.

Signed:

Your name here____________________________

4) The Power of the Word

Genesis, the first book of the Bible, reads: 'In the beginning, the *logos* [the word, or the mind of Christ according to Christians] was God.'[32] With this perspective in mind, the process of creation would have followed these three stages: a thought (mind) that physically self-creates through the word (the verb). Therefore, the uni-verse is a

[32] John 1:1

one-verse, a marvelous sound in unity that is heard through eternity. Such is the power of the word that it can decree, create, and bring love, peace, health, and life into reality. However, it also has the power to destroy, create discord, declare wars, and issue death sentences. You may create a male-diction (evil diction) or a bene-diction (good-diction); you may bless inasmuch as you may curse. Following this same line of ideas, I would add: Be transparent with your words always. Be truthful, with integrity. Do not say things 'just because'. Do not make commitments on which you cannot follow through. Do not say what you do not feel. In colloquial words, say what you mean and mean what you say.

On the other hand, if someone says something about you that is not true, do not believe it. Do not believe in dark voices or those of the ego, nor should you play the game of spreading words about illness, judgment, fear, and hate. Lastly, it is equally important that you never lie to yourself.

5) Prayer

Prayer is our way of asking for help whenever our ship has gone off course. It is our way of sending emergency flares up to the heavens, an SOS signal, so that our request is heard. Prayer is still the best way to ask God for help. You must pray with your heart, feeling each word. All prayers are designed to provide us with peace the minute we say them since they are always heard before spoken. More powerful than asking God for a specific outcome is to ask Him for His Will since He knows the best outcome for you and others before a situation was even created. The highest form of prayer is to *know.* Therefore, prayer must always come with a feeling of certainty and gratitude, using, for example, the words Jesus spoke, and repeating, 'Thank you, Father, for I know You always listen. May Your highest Will be done.'

6) Meditation

If prayer is our tool for asking God, then silence is our tool for receiving His answer. Silence is the necessary frequency inside our radio transmitters to receive His instructions. It is only through stillness that we may receive Divine guidance. Breathing exercises are beneficial to help you reach this calm state. There is also a simple meditation, described below, that is efficient in creating the silence you need to receive your miracle.

PRACTICE: THE RAINBOW MEDITATION

I learned this mediation from Alexander Everett, a dear teacher, considered a teacher of teachers, and co-creator of the Human Potential Movement in the early 70s, the precursor of the Large Awareness Training we see today. He also believed that the one solution to all of our problems lies in connection with God. This meditation will especially help you to be centered. Just as a small comment may affect you for a whole day, being centered is the shield to protect you against being vulnerable to triggers and in the face of adverse situations. Martial arts teaches how to find our center of inner strength before a match because it is practically impossible to knock down a warrior who is 'anchored' to the earth. Likewise, this meditation helps you keep this center. While centered, you will see that challenging situations simply won't knock you out of your center. Whether it is a piece of bad news, an argument with your partner or a curveball that is thrown at you unexpectedly – when you are centered, you are prepared and do not react negatively to unexpected events.

Find a quiet space, close your eyes, and breathe deeply. Let all the worries of the day go. If any thoughts come to mind, just watch and let them go without resistance. On a trip to India, Alexander was identified as a swami by another master from India. The colors of the rainbow are a correlation of the Seven Chakras (in Sanskrit) or energy centers. Imagine a vast rainbow and prepare to ascend and pass through it as if in a shower of colors. Imagine how all the colors of the rainbow cover your entire body.

1. **Red/Your Body:** Begin with the red light, as you visualize a beautifully colored ruby, red like an apple, wrapping your entire body. Meditate and repeat: 'My body is relaxed, calmed.' Experience the feeling of abundance and safety.
2. **Orange/Your Emotions**: Imagine all of your emotional body covered by a brilliant orange light. Meditate and repeat: 'My emotional body is healthy. I am beautiful, attractive, and young. I am sexually healthy. I am creative. I freely express and feel my emotions. I am free from attachments.'
3. **Yellow/Your Mind:** Imagine all of your mental body covered by a brilliant yellow light as you think of the sun and its shining rays. Meditate and repeat: 'My mind is at ease. I take control of my life and my situation

responsibly. I trust myself and others and God. I can create, solve problems, develop solutions and projects, and make decisions. I let go of my control over situations I cannot change, and I let go of the need to control others.'

4. **Green/Love**: Imagine a brilliant green light covering your whole body with love. As you visualize green, think of a green prairie and feel the love beating in your heart. Meditate and repeat within: 'I love and accept others. I love myself; therefore, I can love my neighbors, and my love is returned. My heart is clean. My family relationships are full of love, understanding, and respect. I love within healthy limits, without attachments. I forgive and am forgiven. I am love. God loves me. I feel God's love in my heart.'
5. **Blue/Communication**: Imagine a brilliant blue covering all of your body as you visualize the blue ocean. Meditate and repeat the following phrase within: 'I can communicate my needs without hurting others. I can speak the truth at all times. My word is as good as gold. I have a voice in all circumstances. I can ask and state my needs freely, and I can listen to others and understand them. I understand and am understood. There are no misunderstandings.'
6. **Indigo/Vision**: Imagine a brilliant indigo light covering your body and centered on your third eye. At the same time, visualize the color through a dark, indigo sky at twilight, illuminating you with a ray of light. Meditate and repeat this phrase within: 'God reveals a beautiful vision of my future to me. I see beyond appearances. I

do not judge. I am willing to see things as they are, and the truth to every situation is revealed to me.'

7. **Violet/God's speed.** Imagine a pale violet light covering your body as you visualize a brilliant lilac funnel on top of your crown, with its wide opening towards the sky. Meditate and repeat within: 'I allow myself to receive God's full guidance today. I feel connected to God at all times. May His Will be done in all areas of my life.'

I found that if you do this practice meditation for thirty consecutive days, its sequence stays recorded in your subconscious. From then on, whenever you do not have enough time, you can practice a shorter version for a couple of minutes, which can be just as effective. This shorter version requires only that you imagine the sequence of colors bathing you as it relaxes you.

To end the meditation, repeat this color sequence completely, this time in reverse. Start with the light violet and go all the way to the red. When finished, lightly stretch, and then, when you are ready and consciousness is returning to your body, slowly open your eyes and give thanks putting both hands together in front of your heart.

Meditation has been found to have impressive benefits when practiced daily; since I originally wrote this book, empirical studies have found new evidence for its health benefits. Meditation can:

1. Balance all areas of your life.
2. Avoid sickness.
3. Calm your nervous system.

4. Smooth rough emotions.
5. Ease your mind.
6. Relax your body.
7. Allow your connection with God to stay clear.
8. Improve your vision of life.
9. Give power to your creativity.
10. Elevate your self-esteem.
11. Obtain inner peace.
12. Protect you against depression.

7) Love and Compassion

Everything that we do with love results in excellence. When our actions are contaminated by the need for recognition, our deeds are filled with an unhealthy eagerness to please. Attachment to an outcome brings worries and blame, and our results will manifest the same qualities. When we love another in the form of compassion, it is God using our hands as instruments to lighten the burden of another. When we give from our hearts without expecting anything in return, this is the true meaning of fulfillment.

A loving heart is fast to forgive itself and others, and slow to anger and judge as we learned in the book of Proverbs. When you allow yourself to be guided by love, the path towards your purpose is much easier to walk. There is much talk about excellence and efficiency when providing a service, but in reality, the only ingredient we need in our actions and daily endeavors, is love. The highest form of worship is to do everything with love in an eternal offering to God. Love is seeing God in everything and recognizing His oneness.

He who is rooted in oneness
realizes that I am
in every being; wherever
he goes, he remains in me.

— Bhagavad Gita [6.29–32][33]

Strategy: Good Humor and Optimism

Do not take yourself too seriously. Live life like a game; if you lose a game, although you did your best and ended up with nothing, you can still smile. Live life lightly and with good humor. Don't worry; you will improve your game the next time. Remember that each mistake is only practicing to improve your next move. If you are in a hurry and happen to fall on your face, laugh at yourself, pick yourself up, clean your knees, and continue on your way. The goal in life is to enjoy every hand, those we win, and those we lose. In writing, there is a rule known as 'literary license' that allows writers to every once in a while, break the strict rules of language.

Similarly, you can also allow yourself a license in life from time to time to break away from the rules. For once, do what no one expects from you. Don't take things that seriously and remember that some days you can 'think outside of the box' and 'color outside of the lines'.

8) Your Inner Voice

What is your heart telling you? Do you take the time to listen? Are you listening? If we cannot hear our inner voice,

---

[33] Stephen Mitchell, in Bhagavad Gita: A New Translation (New York: Harmony Books, 2000), p. 92.

silenced by thousands of thoughts and conflicting opinions, we will never know for sure what direction to take in life. We will blame others for choosing for us, and we will not have peace. Don't be afraid to make mistakes; if we do not dare to follow our hearts and act accordingly, we will never grow. Follow your heart. God dwells inside.

Discerning your authentic inner voice

The inner voice is better known as intuition, from the Latin *intueri*, meaning 'to look within'. The inner voice is the voice of God who speaks inside of us. Intuition is different from reason and the mind. It is the language of our Creator, and His voice can only be heard in silence. Maybe even akin to a hum, almost like an eternal lullaby of love. You recognize the authentic voice because it is constant and certain. It is soft but persistent like the steady sound of a drum that won't stop drumming for you, always reminding you to keep moving, that there is an ideal path waiting for you. It does not matter how many mistakes you have made or how many years you have strayed away from your way. The voice inside your heart keeps beating constantly and consistently, reminding you of your true north. This voice in your heart will never talk to you with reproach, will not blame, or make you feel guilty. Once you finally listen to it, you can no longer ignore it, and like a shining sun, it will light your whole being, filling it with hope.

Intuition is seeing beyond mere appearances and listening beyond words. Spiritual senses are analogous to the physical ones, and they give us the ability to go beyond the physical senses' limits (the physical world). Intuition can only be available when you listen to your inner voice and are connected to God.

Discerning the right path

The right path flows like a river; it goes over rocks, and even a mountain of logs won't be able to stop its flow. The ideal path has a mind of its own, makes its own agendas and appointments, introduces you to new people and situations in the direction of your new destiny, bringing you everything it needs and removing all obstacles that will slow you down.

When Mother Teresa sensed a conflict between her dreams and reality, she simply said, 'If this project doesn't come to reality, it is simply because God isn't interested in it.' The right path feels right, and despite your fears and obstacles, a real flame of hope continues to light the way. Even if you miss a turn on your ideal path or lose your way while taking an apparent rest, your voice eventually returns. Your destiny never gives up.

On the other hand, the wrong path does not give you peace, since being utterly faithful to your integrity is the compass that will lead you smoothly through these waters. Never take a path you feel is wrong, even though it seems to promise a bright future. If you have to compromise any of your values, it is not the path for you. When the road is wrong, even if it is paved with gleaming marble, you will know. It is not the right path if it compromises your integrity, if you have to lie to others or yourself, sell yourself at the cost of your values, or hurt others while gaining an advantage. If you need to take something away from others – an opportunity, a possession, peace, or a relationship, this most likely is the wrong way. If there is a price attached to the path, albeit an emotional one, or if you must compromise any of your loved ones, this path is clearly out of harmony for you; therefore, reframe your motivation.

Fear is not the best motivation for making a choice unless you are running away from a tiger. Before taking a new path, question whether this is a new road or just an old one but carefully disguised as new. There is no need to take the wrong path twice. Confirm the right way by questioning whether this new path is genuinely aligned with what God envisions for your future. Lastly, do not forget to ask if an enchanting path that seems certain is just a temptation to enjoy some temporary sensations in exchange for long-standing consequences. For example, the results of having unprotected sex, gambling, buying on impulse, driving while intoxicated, stealing, or taking drugs.

Feel-good sensations and pleasure aren't always signs of being on the right path. Our senses can frequently deceive us.

Listening to your heart

In my case, it's very curious. When I am about to make a wrong decision, my shoulders and neck let me know, for they tighten strangely. In your case, it may be the stomach or the back that revolts. It may be your blood pressure that lets you know. Listen to your inner voice and watch the signs of the body. They will always tell if you are on the right track. Sometimes it is not that apparent; a persistent inner uneasiness will let you know when you are on the wrong path. The voice of intuition never works with blame or negativity about you. In the Spanish language, the word for compass is *compás*, and it sounds like 'con paz', which means 'with peace', so choose the path that gives you the most peace.

Synchronizing with the Will of God

Your dreams and God's dreams are one. First, you sync with your inner voice through silence by breathing, praying, creative visualization, meditation, and contemplation. Maintain the connection with God by becoming aware of His presence. Live in the now and substitute each doubtful, shameful, or painful thought for one of faith and hope. Remember to 'seek first the kingdom of God and His righteousness, and all these things shall be added.'[34] Seek first to find the path God has for you. Dream, flow, choose, and when the signs are so clear that you have no doubts, act, and carry out your tasks with love.

Strategy: How to make a choice

Rather than make a decision, simply make a choice. The word 'decision' comes from cutting, separating, and discarding other possibilities. Therefore, the word is strong and must be used cautiously. The verb 'to choose' is softer and flexible, and it has 'to taste' as its root. It refers to considering several possibilities and selecting among them. There are specific times when sound decisions must be made, such as deciding to quit a habit, an addiction, or a toxic relationship. The rest of the time, it is best to make choices.

---

[34] Matthew 6:33

If you choose, you have possibilities. If you decide, you have one option. Furthermore, this decision could be responsible for many wrongs, even expired agreements being kept for a lifetime, just because they were made under the precept of a *decision*. This does not mean that you may weaken your own word by not having a sense of commitment, with escape clauses, back doors, or hidden agendas.

We can always change our path. If you find yourself walking a path of thorns that becomes impassable, there is no reason to continue, especially if the circumstances have changed or if you feel a strong need to change lanes or even to go back to your original place. We are not talking about being undependable. We are talking about situations in life where delaying a change of route because of an expired agreement could be the worst choice. If we fail to act when we receive our cue, we run the risk of allowing others to make choices for us, releasing us falsely from the responsibility of our actions for fear of making a mistake or failing. Whether a financial investment, a toxic relationship, or a job position, this is about using inner wisdom to make choices based on your present truth rather than reactions to old commitments and wrong beliefs.

> *The hardest lesson in life is learning to choose between which bridge to cross and which bridge to burn.*
>
> — David Russell

In an excellent translation of the Tao, Stephen Mitchell wrote, 'Don't make decisions, let decisions make themselves.'[35] The phrase alludes to allowing God to choose the path for us, by seeing how He eliminates the other alternatives by closing doors. But to see this objectively, we must first completely let go of any stubborn determination to take a specific path, since it may very well be the wrong one. The best would be to allow God to reveal to us a preview of the path ahead of time; in this way, we may avoid wasting time or getting upset.

> *The more I detach myself from what I want, the clearer I can see what I truly need.*

9) We are Not Alone

We live in a world that is material, but we are also part of a parallel, invisible universe where angels live. Angels have been present in our society throughout history. They have been sent to Earth by God to help the planet throughout time. Angels may intervene and step in at any time to help you. They sometimes appear as unexpected support or in the form of a person who helps you, say, to change a flat tire in a dangerous neighborhood in the middle of the night. They may come to give you a warning, like an inexplicable desire to stop your car for no reason, only seconds before a possible accident.

Believe in Angels

The Archangel Michael is considered the chief commander of Heaven. According to various traditions He has interceded for humanity in numerous occasions.

---

[35] Stephen Mitchell, *The Second Book of the Tao: Compiled and Adapted from the Chuang-Tzu and the Chung Yung, with Commentaries* (New York: Penguin Books, 2010).

A simple prayer to invoke the protection of angels every morning, it is also good for children.

PRAYER TO SAINT MICHAEL THE ARCHANGEL

(Point with your finger as you say it)
Saint Michael, protect me:
Saint Michael, before me, Saint Michael, behind me,
Saint Michael, above me, Saint Michael, below me,
Saint Michael, on my right side, Saint Michael, on my left side,
Everywhere I go, Saint Michael is beside me.

Finish the prayer giving thanks and bringing your hands to your heart.

Orange butterflies and other fairies

One night, I had an unusual encounter. I saw a gigantic butterfly flying in my garden. She showed up suddenly, and although she did not stay long, I enjoyed her visit with all my heart and still vividly remember her. I kept telling myself, 'I have never seen an orange butterfly come to this house in the eight years I have been living here, least of all at night.' It is uncommon to see a diurnal butterfly at night, yet it happened, and I have witnessed the event. I did not take that visit lightly. It was undoubtedly a message I was later able to decipher: an omen of the beginning of a new rebirth in my life.

Messages from above

Has it happened to you – a message seems to come to you straight from the heavens? Maybe you felt your loved one in the breeze after his passing, telling you he was well and living in the light. Perhaps it was a time you fell in love, and suddenly the song on the radio confirmed your suspicion. Messages from above are subtle ways for God to communicate good news. The language is magical, filled with colors, hope, and love. I believe that the spirit of God lives in nature, in the animals and the wind. Frequently they become assistants to bring His messages from Heaven. All we need to do is be awake enough to be able to decode their everyday nuances.

Signs of nature

I remember one beautiful afternoon I was driving along a narrow countryside road in Italy. We were enjoying the view when suddenly an impressive blackbird crossed in front of our car. I immediately felt an uneasy cold. Unable to contain myself, I screamed, 'Watch out!' and so we did, only to witness the hair-raising scene of an accident some seconds later, between a vehicle and a cyclist, whose corpse was covered by a white cloth. I still have to figure out the full meaning of this message. Maybe it prevented us from running over the cyclist, or perhaps it was the angel of death, who came to take a soul and also remind us that life is short.

Another sign occurred on the road in Miami, where I found myself surrounded by fog, shortly after I had begun writing this book on how God guides us through the dark.

I kept saying, 'I live in Miami. It is not normal to have fog on the roads here,' and I asked God and His angels to clear my path. I returned home safely but kept wondering about the meaning behind that sudden fog. Two days later, a nebulous situation in my life, one involving lies and deceit, was revealed to me.

Everything that happens outside is a reflection of our inner world; we just need to learn to interpret God's symbolic language in our lives. Sudden events are His language, the symbols are His letters, and the feelings aroused by the events are the tone of the messages. Any Divine message must be translated into our hearts. Meditation, voluntarily connecting with God, and daily periods of silence have all awakened a beautiful experience in me: to be able to recognize and decipher this foreign language at least part of the time.

THE STRANGE BLUE BUTTERFLY

I met Marina during a trip to Panama. She is one of those beings of light you meet on your path. After our encounter, she gifted me a Blue Morpho butterfly's miniature replica, an icon of her native country Costa Rica. The wings in these Morpho butterflies are covered with crystalline scales that shine in blue and green shades when the sunlight hits them. However, when the butterfly rests, the only part you will see is a brown silhouette. When the wings are closed, you will never imagine her beautiful blue color. The brown is her natural camouflage strategy to protect herself among the trees. When Marina gave me her gift, she told me I was like one of those Morpho butterflies. She said that I needed to come out of hiding and open my wings to show my best colors. 'You are a being of light covered under the shadows of a sad past, but now it's time to show your true colors and share a message of hope to the world.'

The blue butterfly is considered a magical being; legend has it that whoever can catch a Blue Morpho receives a miracle. The blue butterfly on the cover of the first Spanish edition of my book is the same one Marina gave me years ago when I still did not know that I was going to write it. What does your blue butterfly look like? What are the messages that God is sending to you? Can you see them now? Stay alert. Your answers may be closer than you think.

10) The Will

We will need a superhuman will to keep our integrity and loyalty focused on the Divine plan at all times. A will surrendered to God's is the most powerful secret weapon you can possess. A strong will is made with persistence, which is not the same as insistence. Perseverance is a loving commitment, whereas insistence is the ego attached to immediate results.

Strategy: Effort instead of struggle

We are trained to fight from an early age. Sayings like 'no pain, no gain' or 'you must fight for what you want' are prevalent in our world. Struggling and fighting are the national hymns in our modern society, forever proud to be engaged in a battle. There is a general belief that if things are running too smoothly, something must be wrong. We feel that to get ahead, we must fight and struggle, words related to quarreling and dispute – and that is how we spend our lives most of the time. Are battles and suffering our natural state of being?

Once again, nature's example shows us the way. One day, I was sitting in the garden with my daughter watching a bird make a nest. Ever determined, the bird would fly to the tree time after time with twigs in its beak to weave them into a nest. Sometimes the work was in vain, for the twig would fall from its beak, almost at the end of every other flight. The little bird did not give up, though. We counted dozens of flights with no apparent result on the nest's side. Was the little bird suffering? Was it struggling? Nature gives us everything we need, like the twigs for the bird's nest and the instinct to build it. Building the nest meant a considerable amount of effort for the bird, but it was far from suffering or struggling. Lions must run and try to catch their prey, but they are agile enough to do so. Likewise, we must know the tools we have and acquire additional ones to live without suffering and struggle.

A situation persists if you resist it, but it loses power if you accept it. Responsibility is not the same as blame. It is the art of responding to life accordingly. The negative feelings you harbor are yours, and it is you who gives them power. The meaning of suffering is to resist, to deny, and to hold on. Letting go and accepting, both free you from suffering.

The law of least resistance is expressed in nature. The water of an ever-flowing river never fights an obstacle. When it encounters a rock, it doesn't stop; it doesn't resist. It only embraces the rock to later continue its voyage. When something does not come out well, when it does not flow regardless of our effort, then it is time to reevaluate the situation and take another route. Maybe it is not the right time or the right way. Perhaps we need more tools, more information, or more strength. There is a time for everything. State what you need, but do not waste time defending your position. If there is no receptivity on the other side, you will probably waste time and energy since we are seldom able to convince another to change. And if you do succeed, but it causes more suffering, then let it go and continue on. Do not persist. Choose your battles wisely. Most of them nowadays are just a waste of energy.

11) Non-attachment

Non-attachment is one of the most powerful weapons you may use. Healthy non-attachment is, as we observed earlier in nature, letting the water flow without interfering. Hopeless attachment is the most significant cause of wars, deaths, destruction, and separation. When you have no possessions, no nationalistic pride, no one will be able to manipulate or declare war against you. When you allow God to be the only source of your strength, not depending on outside sources, nothing and no one can make you tumble. Non-attachment precedes non-violence; justice is the realization of Oneness.

12) Faith

Being connected to God is undoubtedly the most powerful tool of all. God is the ultimate constant source of inner peace. Far from meaning blind belief in something, the word 'faith' comes from the Latin *fides*, meaning 'loyal'. We find 'fides' as the root in many words of strength like 'bona fides', 'fidelity', and 'confidence'. You can only be faithful to something you genuinely believe in and love with all your being. Our faith is nurtured by our loyalty to God, above all material and fleeting possessions of this world. Having faith means to trust entirely in God and the masterful Order of His Will. Faith is believing – without the crutch of evidence – that He will respond.

SUMMARY OF THE CONNECTION PROCESS

1) Observe yourself

Stop for a moment on your path and observe yourself. Breathe deeply several times until you are relaxed. Do not react. Stay silent and observe the situation presented to you. Do not make any decisions in the heat of the moment. Keep silent and begin the communion with God so that He may guide you, and you may see through His eyes.

2) Accept

Accept and come to terms with your present results, since everything you resist will get stronger. Acceptance is not giving up, rather it is being responsible and acting with a positive and proactive aim, always exercising self-control over your reactions. Humbly accept the place where you are on the path, without denial or blame. Consciously knowing where you are on the road is enough for you to determine the direction you should turn to next.

3) Be grateful

Give thanks for every lesson you receive, since each fall houses a miracle. By thanking God, you let Him know that you are ready to receive His miracles. Everything happens for a reason. Remember that even stars and galaxies have an order ruling them.

4) Ask for Divine Will

Consciously inviting and asking for Divine assistance means allowing God to inspire us with a solution that can be applied to any situation. Now we understand that we all have free will, the most significant gift and that not even God will interfere with that right unless consciously invited. God always has the perfect answer; the secret lies in granting Him permission to come in and assist us. If we do not willingly allow God to come into our lives to take on our challenges, His help might be delayed.

THE CONNECTION PRAYER

My Father, I call upon Your Celestial Presence so that it may be present in my whole being at all times. I allow Your Will to be done in all areas of my life. At this moment and always, I allow all of your wisdom to work through me. I invite your Higher Will to guide, bless and, protect all of my personal relationships, my family, my finances, my purpose, my health, my physical surroundings, my service, and my spirituality. I surrender my mind, thoughts, emotions, and spirit to Your Wisdom, so that You may harmonize them in Your Light. I accept becoming an instrument of Your

Plan through Your Will, expressing this way my highest potential through Your Presence within me. Use me in ways unimaginable to me. Make me an instrument of Your Plan; take my talents, hands, voice, eyes, ears, brain, legs, and imagination, and bless them with Your Highest Will of love. Amen!

5) Forgive

When we forgive ourselves, we love ourselves, and when we forgive others, we are freed. Some faults are unforgivable at first sight, and so the only way to truly 'forgive' is with the help of God's Divine grace. We realize that only we can give the power away for an act against us to hurt eternally. Forgiving is different from excusing another's actions. It recognizes that nothing or no one can hurt you without your consent. Pray: 'My God, I am willing to forgive through You.'

6) Let go and let God

You must release the situation entirely, let it go, and let God enter into it without expecting any outcome or solution and without waiting for specific reactions from people. Eradicate your attachment to a result. If you can trust and detach yourself from the situation, you will see how the fear, blame, and unleashed anger ultimately give way to God's intelligence and self-compassion. The same intelligence will move all the planets in the universe to solve your problem. Non-attachment is not a form of martyrdom. It is not resignation or inactivity. It is an act of responsibility.

7) Spread the message

To keep this inner peace and connection everlasting, you must carry out the last step in the Connection Process: sharing with others and helping others find their relationship with God, not through preaching or trying to convince them, but through the natural expression of your new being. When someone asks you about your inner peace, that is the perfect time to share, granting all recognition for your talents, gifts, and success to their real source: God.

PRACTICE: DAILY EXERCISES

The person you are today is the result of thousands of little choices and decisions made daily. The sum of all the moments you have experienced brought you here now. If unaware, your opportunities to make these valuable daily choices will slip through your hands, given that they are not necessarily made up of giant steps or great heroic acts. Instead, these are small and constant steps that will lead to the ideal in the different areas of your life. Today you may begin by taking the small steps (given below) towards a conscious, harmonious, and connected life: a life guided by a purpose in every aspect of your existence.

> *No problem can be solved from the same level of consciousness that created it.*
>
> — Albert Einstein

Reminder for your daily practices

This guide does not require you to follow a specific order. You may adapt it and modify it according to your immediate priorities and situations. There is no perfect way to use it. Remember that life is made up of present moments; therefore, it is essential to continue enjoying every day in fulfilling ways as your challenges continue to take care of themselves because the present is perfect. It is the result of the best decisions you could have made based on your level of consciousness. This frame of mind eliminates judgment and allows you to live fully. This does not mean we are not going to do what is possible to improve our lives. It means that while we are growing, we can continue to 'live fully'.

Daily practices

- Silence and self-examination
- Meditation
- Connection Process
- Presence
- One step for your physical body
- One step for your abundance
- One step for your spirituality
- One step for your service
- One step for your personal relationships
- One step for your family relationships
- One step for your true purpose

EPILOGUE: A NEW SEASON

MY DEEPEST WISH IS THAT BEGINNING TODAY, AND AS A result of this book, you choose to live with the certainty of being protected, confident amidst the uncertainties of these troubling times filled with sickness, wars, tribulations, and catastrophes. I wish that you continue centered in your purpose, far from fears, and planted firmly on the path God has planned for you. I assure you, once again, that while you are in His Company, you will always be protected from all adversity. A new cycle is beginning, a rebirth for humanity, not destruction. The future is not written. We will paint it with our intentions, actions, thoughts, and imagination.

Will we be able to visualize a new world in peace? Live with enthusiasm. Spend time in silence. Take care of your thoughts. Feel your emotions. Look into the light. Simplify your life. Play with a child. Smile. Watch nature. Leave a legacy. Plant a tree. Lift someone. Forgive someone. Dance. Love someone. Ask for forgiveness and grant yours. Act, don't be afraid of making mistakes. Live here and now. Learn from your lessons. Live your passion, and do not be immobilized by your fears. Don't complain about what has already passed. Enjoy every moment of your life. Do all these with love and in the company of God, and your life will forever flow in peace, regardless of external circumstances.

ACKNOWLEDGMENTS

I HUMBLY THANK GOD AND HIS ANGELS FOR PROVIDING all the light, the love, and the patience to this reluctant and imperfect seeker. Gabbie, thank you for lending your mom to the universe; you are my blessing.

I am especially grateful to Prasun Chatterjee, Editorial Director and to Rajdeep Mukherjee, Managing Director, of Pan Macmillan Publishing India, for the opportunity for this work to be published in India, an immense honor.

To Jayleen Gorritz, my soul sister, thank you – without our endless conversations, this book would not be in the hands of the readers. Martha Daza, thank God for your brushstrokes in the editing of the original Spanish version. Your clear and unconditional guidance gave me the certainty that these thoughts were in a rational and coherent order. Thank you, Juli Peradejordi, for the first opportunity and to you, Giovanna Cuccia, for believing in this message – despite living on different continents. Every time you cross my path, a miracle occurs. Thank you, J.P. Dada Vaswani, my teacher, now in Heaven; thank you for showing me the face of God. How you came to me from India to Puerto Rico is a mystery. Thank you,

Larry Downs, for all your wise words and encouragement. Grateful to you Montse Cortazar, my literary agent for international rights, for giving wings to this book. Much appreciation to Emmanuel Cavazos and Josué Rivas for your unending support. A book is as good as the work of a wonderful team, and I am lucky to have one. Thanks to you Teresita Zamora, for laying the first canvas of this translation. Over the years I painted some of my own words in a new language with the help of Ginny Killfoile. Thank you Ginny, for all the updates and corrections as the new editions were published. Grateful also to Elizabeth James for the last corrections; you placed your golden seal on this work.

I am grateful to everyone who contributed to my learning and the dissemination of these teachings.